HARMONY

KEY TO
CHADWICK'S HARMONY

Da Capo Press Music Reprint Series
ROLAND JACKSON
GENERAL EDITOR

HARMONY
A Course of Study

and

A KEY TO
CHADWICK'S HARMONY

by

G. W. Chadwick

DA CAPO PRESS • NEW YORK • 1975

Library of Congress Cataloging in Publication Data

Chadwick, George Whitefield, 1854-1931.
    Harmony: a course of study and A Key to Chadwick's
harmony.

    (Da Capo Press music reprint series)
    Reprint of 1st editions, 1897 and 1902, published by
B. F. Wood, Boston.
    1. Harmony. I. Chadwick, George Whitefield, 1854-
1931. A key to Chadwick's Harmony. 1975.
MT50.C43   1975   781.3   74-36316
ISBN 0-306-70663-6

This Da Capo Press edition of *Harmony* is an unabridged republication of the first edition published in Boston in 1897 to which is appended *A Key to Chadwick's Harmony* reproduced from the first edition published in Boston in 1902. *Harmony* is reprinted from an original in the collections of the Vassar College Library. *A Key to Chadwick's Harmony* is reprinted from an original in the collections of the Memorial Library, University of Wisconsin.

Published by Da Capo Press, Inc.
A Subsidiary of Plenum Publishing Corporation
227 West 17th Street, New York, N.Y. 10011

HARMONY

A COURSE OF STUDY

BY

G. W. CHADWICK, A.M.

DIRECTOR OF THE NEW ENGLAND CONSERVATORY OF MUSIC

BOSTON, MASS.

———

BOSTON
THE B. F. WOOD MUSIC CO.

F. H. GILSON COMPANY,
PRINTERS AND BOOKBINDERS,
BOSTON, U. S. A.

PREFACE.

The object of this book is to give the student a working vocabulary of chords for the harmonizing of melodies in the order of their practical value and harmonic importance. The author has endeavored to encourage the student to use his ever-increasing chord material,— not so much by warnings against what is bad, as by examples of what is good, as musicians understand it, and by maxims deduced from such examples.

This book is not intended to deprive the teacher of his occupation, but rather to furnish him with useful text and material, systematically arranged, which he is to illustrate and elucidate as much as is necessary. To this end copious references and elaborate explanations of details have been avoided as much as is consistent with lucid statement.

The student is supposed to have already a rudimentary knowledge of the intervals, scales and chords given in the introduction.

THE AUTHOR.

CONTENTS.

INTRODUCTORY.

SCALES, INTERVALS, AND CHORDS.

MAJOR SCALES.

The succession of tones C D E F G A B C, called the **scale of C major, or natural scale,** is the form on which the major scales of all other keys are modeled. The distance between the tones is as follows:

$$C \; \tfrac{1}{1} \; D \; \tfrac{1}{1} \; E \; \tfrac{1}{2} \; F \; \tfrac{1}{1} \; G \; \tfrac{1}{1} \; A \; \tfrac{1}{1} \; B \; \tfrac{1}{2} \; C.$$
$$1 \qquad 2 \qquad 3 \qquad 4 \qquad 5 \qquad 6 \qquad 7 \qquad 8$$

That is to say, between 3 and 4, 7 and 8 are half tones; between all the others consecutively, whole tones.

The names of the degrees or steps of the scale are: tonic, supertonic, mediant, subdominant, dominant, submediant, and leading tone. The major scale is called diatonic, i.e., it progresses from degree to degree throughout its compass.

While only the signatures of seven sharp and seven flat keys are used in practice besides the natural one, the major scale may be formed on any given tone by the use of double flats and sharps — twenty-six keys in all.

To form a major scale on any given tone write the following formula over the keynote, here indicated by x:

$$\underset{x}{1} \; \tfrac{1}{1} \; 2 \; \tfrac{1}{1} \; 3 \; \tfrac{1}{2} \; 4 \; \tfrac{1}{1} \; 5 \; \tfrac{1}{1} \; 6 \; \tfrac{1}{1} \; 7 \; \tfrac{1}{2} \; 8$$

and then fill in the notes required by the fractions.

MINOR SCALES.

The harmonic minor scale differs from the major in that its **third** and **sixth** degrees are minor instead of major. The diatonic succession is therefore:

$$1 \; \tfrac{1}{1} \; 2 \; \tfrac{1}{2} \; 3 \; \tfrac{1}{1} \; 4 \; \tfrac{1}{1} \; 5 \; \tfrac{1}{2} \; 6 \; \tfrac{3}{2} \; 7 \; \tfrac{1}{2} \; 8$$

This scale contains the same tones (with the exception of the leading tone) as the major scale whose keynote is its third, and is therefore nearest to it in point of tonality.   Hence the term **relative** or **parallel** keys.   The minor scales are formed in the same manner as the major, using the above formula.

The melodic minor scale is not used, strictly speaking, for harmonic purposes (see Lesson 40), but may be here given as a matter of general knowledge.   Its sixth and seventh degrees are major in ascending and minor in descending, the third of course being minor in both cases.

INTERVALS.

The difference in pitch which separates two tones, whether in combination or succession, is called an **interval**.   This term is also applied to the association of the tones themselves in regard to pitch; i.e., we say that F to C is a fifth, whereas we mean that the distance between them is a fifth.

Intervals are counted upward from the lower to the higher, and are named

First, from the number of degrees of the scale which they occupy, and

Second, from the number of tones and semitones which they contain.

Thus to find the general or numerical name of any interval we put ourselves into the *major key* of its lower tone.   Its higher tone then occupies the degree of the scale from which the interval is named; thus,

The *general* or *numerical* name of intervals applies to their *visible* difference in size, and is not affected by any number of accidentals before their lower or upper tones.

The *specific* name of intervals refers partly to the chromatic modification of the diatonic (normal) intervals of the scale, and partly to their qualities as concords and discords; thus,

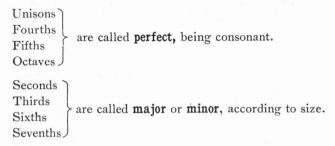

Unisons ⎫
Fourths ⎬ are called **perfect,** being consonant.
Fifths ⎪
Octaves ⎭

Seconds ⎫
Thirds ⎬ are called **major** or **minor,** according to size.
Sixths ⎪
Sevenths ⎭

Any interval may be expanded by accidentals into an **augmented,** or contracted into a **diminished** interval.

A perfect or major interval is augmented by **one** chromatic semitone.

A perfect or minor interval is diminished by **one** chromatic semitone.

NOTE. A second or ninth when diminished is called enharmonic — that is, two different notations of the same pitch.

A major interval is diminished by **two** chromatic semitones.

A minor interval is augmented by **two** chromatic semitones.

Perfect. Augmented. Minor. Diminished.   Major. Diminished.   Minor. Augmented.

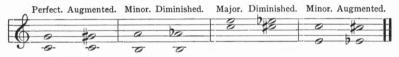

All the natural (normal) intervals of a major scale, counting upward from its tonic (keynote), are either major or perfect.

Intervals greater than the ninth are named the same as those within the compass of the octave.

The concords and discords are classified as follows:

Perfect unisons ⎫
Perfect fourths ⎬ **perfect consonances.**
Perfect fifths ⎪
Perfect octaves ⎭

Major and minor thirds ⎫ **imperfect consonances.**
Major and minor sixths ⎭

Major and minor seconds ⎫
Major and minor sevenths ⎬ **dissonances.**
and all augmented and di- ⎪
   minished intervals ⎭

Dissonances must be resolved, i. e., followed by consonances.
By inversion

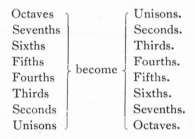

Octaves ⎫   ⎧ Unisons.
Sevenths ⎪   ⎪ Seconds.
Sixths ⎪   ⎪ Thirds.
Fifths ⎪   ⎪ Fourths.
   ⎬ become ⎨
Fourths ⎪   ⎪ Fifths.
Thirds ⎪   ⎪ Sixths.
Seconds ⎪   ⎪ Sevenths.
Unisons ⎭   ⎩ Octaves.

Major intervals become minor.
Minor intervals become major.
Augmented intervals become diminished.
Diminished intervals become augmented.

But   Perfect consonances remain perfect consonances.
      Imperfect consonances remain imperfect consonances.
      Dissonances remain dissonances.

To find the name of any interval:
Regard the lower tone as the tonic (keynote) of a major scale.
Count the degrees to the upper tone. If the upper tone corresponds
to the diatonic degree of the scale, the interval is either **major** or
perfect.
If it is greater by a half tone the interval is augmented.
If it is smaller by a half tone the interval is diminished or minor.
If it is greater by two half tones the interval is doubly augmented.
If it is smaller by two half tones the interval is diminished.
In case the lower tone is not a possible keynote of a major scale,
raise or lower it by an accidental to the nearest practicable tonic.
Then raise or lower the upper tone of the interval the same distance;
in both cases without altering the letters.

CHORDS.

A chord is a combination of three or more tones, erected in thirds on a given tone, or derived by transposition from such a combination.

Thus 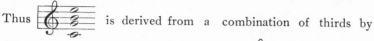 is derived from a combination of thirds by

transposing the upper tone an octave lower  .

A chord with **three** different tones is called a **triad.**

A chord with **four** different tones is called a seventh chord (chord of the seventh).

A chord with **five** different tones is called a ninth chord (chord of the ninth).

The number of parts in a chord may be increased by doubling any of its intervals. This does not alter its character as a triad (three fold), seventh chord (four fold), or ninth chord (five fold).

Triad with root doubled.   Seventh chord with root doubled.   Ninth chord with root doubled.

Chords are designated by the name of the degree of the scale upon which they are founded (tonic, dominant, subdominant, etc.), and this tone is called the **root** of the chord.

When this tone is in the bass the chord is said to be in the **fundamental position.** When any other tone is in the bass the chord is said to be **inverted.**

In vocal music the voices from the highest to the lowest are named as follows:

    Soprano

        Alto

            Tenor

                Bass

and their respective (average) compasses are

Soprano.   Alto.   Tenor.   Bass.

When the three upper voices of a chord lie so closely together that no other interval of the same chord can be placed between them the chord is said to be in **close position.*** Otherwise it is in **open position.**

A major third and perfect fifth constitute a major triad.

A minor third and perfect fifth constitute a minor triad.

A major third and augmented fifth constitute an augmented triad.

A minor third and diminished fifth constitute a diminished triad.

All major and minor triads are **consonant.**

The **first inversion** of a **triad** is called the **chord of the sixth.**

The **second inversion** of a **triad** is called the **chord of the sixth and fourth.**

The **first inversion** of a **seventh chord** is called the **chord of the sixth and fifth.**

The **second inversion** of a **seventh chord** is called the **chord of the fourth and third.**

The **third inversion** of a **seventh chord** is called the **chord of the second, or sixth, fourth, and second.**

All tones which form combinations not derived from the system of thirds above mentioned are called **nonharmonic** or **unessential** tones, and their function is melodic rather than harmonic.

---

* In this case the three upper voices are within the compass of one octave.

HARMONY.

LESSON I.

THE PRINCIPAL TRIADS OF THE MAJOR SCALE.

The principal triads of the major scale are those founded upon the tonic, subdominant and dominant.   As these triads contain every tone of the scale, it is evident that a melody that is strictly diatonic may be harmonized with these chords alone, provided that they can be made to progress from one to another legitimately.

In the study of harmony as an art, two principles are of the most importance :

First, the proper selection and arrangement of the chords which accompany a given melody ;

Second, the proper succession or, as it is called, progression of such chords among themselves.

I. SELECTION OF CHORDS.

Inasmuch as all chords are formed originally by adding the third, fifth, seventh, and ninth to a given bass tone (see Introduction), it follows that in harmonizing any given melody the bass tone is first to be found, and the chord built upon it.   Thus the tones of the major scale will be harmonized as follows, using only the principal triads :

EXPLANATION.

I. **1.** Root of the tonic or fifth of the subdominant.   **2.** Fifth of the dominant.   **3.** Third of the tonic.   **4.** Root of the subdominant. **5.** Fifth of the tonic, or root of the dominant.   **6.** Third of the subdominant.   **7.** Third of the dominant.   From this it will be seen that only three bass tones are needed to harmonize all the tones of the scale.

II. The root (bass tone) appears twice in such chords.

NOTE. It is said to be doubled. The root is always to be doubled for the present in the fundamental position of the principal triads.

III. The chords appear with either root, third, or fifth at the top, but always with the root at the bottom.

NOTE. The position of the triad will be referred to according to the intervals in the soprano voice, i.e., root position, third position, fifth position.

IV. The first and fifth degrees of the scale have two possible harmonizings, while all the others have but one. This is the beginning of the principle of selection referred to above. (See Paragraph I.)

2. CHORD PROGRESSION.

First — The progression of two voices in the same direction is called **parallel motion**. This usually takes place when some other voice becomes a connecting link between two chords.

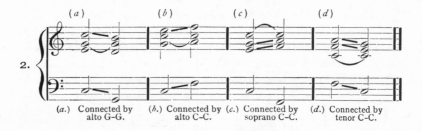

(a.) Connected by alto G–G. (b.) Connected by alto C–C. (c.) Connected by soprano C–C. (d.) Connected by tenor C–C.

Second — The progression of two voices in opposite directions is called **contrary motion**. This takes place when chords having no tone in common succeed one another.

Third — **Oblique motion** (which is not really progression at all, excepting in one voice) is the movement of a voice in any direction against a stationary tone.

It is obvious that oblique motion must always exist whenever a connecting tone is present between two chords.

As in all harmonic progressions the smoothness and simplicity of the voices is a desideratum, such progressions as the following are undesirable:

A chord may be repeated, however, in another of its positions.

On general principles the progression of a given chord is to the nearest position of the next chord, and not to a more distant one, utilizing, if possible, a tone common to both chords, and moving the soprano, alto, and tenor in contrary motion to the bass when such tone is not available.

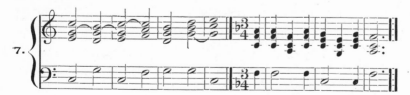

The tones of a melody often suggest, by their progression, the
harmony which underlies them.

For harmonizing the succeeding exercises, the following rules will
be sufficient:

RULE 1.   *When the melody contains successive tones of the same
chord, do not change the harmony (bass tone), but only the position
of the chord.   But if a tone of the melody is* **repeated**, *change the
harmony — especially if the repeated note is on the first beat of the
measure.*

RULE 2.   *Unless one tone is common between two different chords,
move the bass in contrary motion to the three upper voices.*

This involves also another faulty progression, viz.: the skip of a
seventh in the bass.   (See Rule 3.)

RULE 3. *Avoid two fourths or two fifths in succession in the bass, also the skip of a seventh in either direction.* (See Example 10.)

The skip of an octave is, on the contrary, of excellent effect.

NOTE. These progressions are unmelodious, and are easily avoided; thus,

A triad is indicated by the figures **8-5-3**, abbreviated to **8** or **5** or **3**. These figures indicate the intervals which lie in the soprano when the bass is given.

The fundamental harmonies of each degree of the major scale are indicated as follows:

> Tonic.
> Supertonic.
> Mediant.
> Subdominant.
> Dominant.
> Submediant.
> Leading Tone.

The chords which are major are indicated by large numerals, and all others by small. The diminished fifth of the leading tone triad is indicated by the sign °, (thus vII°). For the present we have only to do with I, IV, and V.

All the given models are to be studied systematically as follows:

1. Study the model carefully, without the pianoforte.
2. Write out the bass, add the upper voices, and compare.
3. Write out the soprano, add the other voices, and compare.
4. Play the model from the bass only.
5. Play the model from the soprano only.

I   V   I   I   IV   IV   I   V   V   I IV IV I   I IV   I

a.   Connecting tone.
b.   Change of position in same chord.
c.   Change of harmony with repeated note.

The musical student is cautioned not to write the *fifth in the bass* with the **tonic** triad. Mark Roman numerals under each chord, as in the example given. Write the three upper voices on the upper staff and carefully avoid incorrect notation.

EXERCISES TO LESSON I.

LESSON II.

THE PRINCIPAL TRIADS OF THE MAJOR SCALE.

(Continued.)

In the foregoing lesson the subdominant and dominant triads have been invariably preceded and succeeded by that of the tonic. The succession, subdominant to dominant and dominant to subdominant, has been avoided, not because it is in itself faulty, but because the melody to be harmonized has not rendered it necessary.

As we have no tone in common between the subdominant and dominant triads, we must progress according to Rule 2, Lesson I. Progression by parallel motion between chords in the fundamental position, having no tone in common, involves

First, **consecutive parallel fifths.**

Soprano and tenor, D–G, move in parallel motion to C–F respectively.

Second, **consecutive parallel octaves.**

Tenor and bass, G–G, move in parallel motion to F–F respectively.

Both of these errors are avoided by observing Rule 2. The progression of the subdominant and dominant in such positions is as follows:

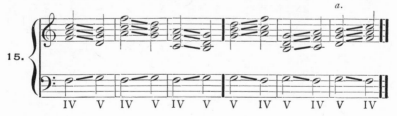

The last progression of dominant and subdominant (see Example 15, *a*) is invariably to be avoided.

RULE 1. *The dominant triad is always succeeded by that of the tonic (never by that of the subdominant), when its third (leading tone) is in the upper voice.*

RULE 2. *In harmonizing a given* **bass** *keep all common tones in the same voices.*

Not because these progressions are incorrect, but because with a given bass they are not necessary.

EXERCISES TO LESSON II.

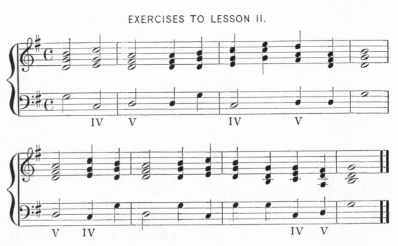

The above model illustrates the progression of V and IV.

NOTE. The root of the first chord is in the upper voice unless otherwise indicated.

1. Bass given.

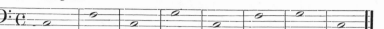

2.

3.

4.

5. Soprano given.

6.

CADENCES.

The succession dominant to tonic triad, with the tonic on the accent, is called the **authentic cadence.** (Example 18, *a*). The succession subdominant to tonic, with the tonic on the accent, is called the **plagal cadence.** (Example 18, *b*.) The succession subdominant, dominant, and tonic, is called the **complete cadence.** (Example 18, *c*.) These successions are used, generally speaking, at the end of a piece, and if the tonic triad appears with the root in the soprano and

bass, the cadences are said to be **perfect**. If with any other interval in either soprano or bass they are said to be **imperfect**.

THE PERFECT CADENCES IN C MAJOR.

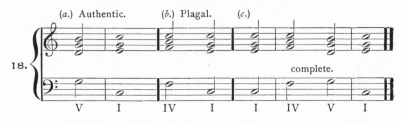

Play the perfect cadences in every major key.

LESSON III.

THE PRINCIPAL TRIADS OF THE MINOR SCALE.

The harmonizing of melodies in the minor mode involves no **new**
principle. In harmonizing the exercises the raised leading tone
must not be overlooked. In a figured bass, it is indicated by a ♯
or ♮ over the dominant of the key.

EXERCISES TO LESSON III.

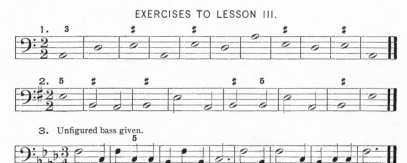

Play the following cadences in every minor key.

LESSON IV.

THE CHORD OF THE SIXTH.

If the third or fifth of a triad, instead of the root, appears in the bass, the triad is said to be inverted:

Root.   Third.

Although a chord when inverted consists of the same tones as in its fundamental position, yet its intervals from the bass are radically changed, and from these intervals the chord receives its name: thus,

From the bass tone the tenor is an octave, the alto a third, the soprano a sixth, hence, **8-3-6,** or chord of the sixth. The removal of the bass from the root to the third of the chord results in the doubling of the third, which we may obviate by removing the alto from the third to the root, thus leaving us with two roots, as in the fundamental position.

The triad, however, when inverted, doubles the fifth or root with equal frequency, and under certain circumstances the third also.

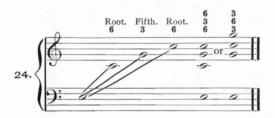

The first inversion of a triad is figured $\frac{8}{6}$ or $\frac{6}{3}$ or **6**. These figures applied to the Roman numerals indicate both the fundamental harmony and its inversions, i.e.

In harmonizing the exercises of this lesson the same rules apply as in the previous one. Only the roots and fifths of the chord of the sixth will be doubled, and in harmonizing basses the connecting tones are to be strictly observed.

NOTE. In case of **two** possible connecting tones on the first or fifth degree of the scale, the **lower** tone is usually the better to retain.

Some available progressions of the chord of the sixth in this lesson are as follows:

Possible combinations for harmonizing the different degrees of the scale are as now follows:

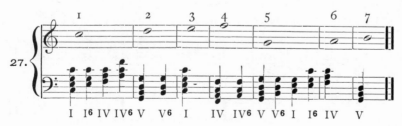

From this it will be seen that we now have three more bass tones at our disposal in the harmonizing of melodies.

EXERCISES TO LESSON IV.

The triads are very often succeeded and preceded by their own inversions.

Incorrect notation is to be carefully avoided.

Play these complete cadences in every major and minor key.

LESSON V.

THE CHORD OF THE SIXTH AND FOURTH.

The second inversion of a triad is called the chord of the sixth and fourth. It is formed by placing the fifth of the triad in the bass.

29.
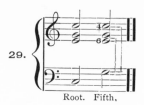

Root. Fifth,

The bass tone of the chord of the sixth and fourth is usually doubled. Chords of the sixth and fourth of the tonic, subdominant, and dominant, may be introduced as follows:

RULE 1. *When preceded and succeeded by a triad in the fundamental position on the same bass tone, or its octave.*

30.

RULE 2. *As the second chord of a group with three ascending or descending bass tones.*

31.

For the present the chord of the sixth and fourth of the dominant only is available for this progression.

In this case the tones of the $\frac{6}{4}$ chord are hardly to be considered as harmonic, but rather as melodic passing tones.

RULE 3. *As a repetition of the same harmony, forming a melodic bass.*

NOTE. These three rules may perhaps be summed up as follows : Avoid skips to or from the bass of a $\frac{6}{4}$ chord. The bass is either stationary or diatonic when the harmony changes.

The principal function of the tonic $\frac{6}{4}$ chord is to precede the dominant chord in the authentic cadence. In fact, the formula $I\frac{6}{4}$–V–I, stereotyped as it is, may be perhaps considered the most useful, as well as the most decided of all authentic forms of cadence. It is used in all the following exercises of this lesson.

All other $\frac{6}{4}$ chords are practically melodic rather than harmonic. It is hardly necessary to state that a piece never begins nor ends with a $\frac{6}{4}$ chord.

EXERCISES TO LESSON V.

a. Rule 1. *b.* Rule 3.

Play these cadences in every major and minor key.

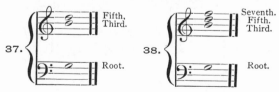

I   IV   I$^6_4$ V   I

LESSON VI.

THE CHORD OF THE DOMINANT SEVENTH.

By adding a seventh to the triad on the fifth degree of the scale, a chord is formed called the **dominant seventh**.

Inasmuch as the seventh is a **dissonance** (see Introduction), it must be followed by a certain tone demanded by the ear, which is called its **resolution.** As this tone is the third of the tonic triad, and as the fifth degree of the scale on which the dominant seventh chord is founded is common to both tonic and dominant chords, the third and fifth of the dominant seventh chord have only to progress to the root of the tonic to form a complete tonic chord.

NOTE. The dominant seventh chord consists of a major third, perfect fifth, and minor seventh. This combination of intervals is only to be found on the fifth degree of the scale, and is the same in both major and minor keys.

RULES FOR THE USE OF THE DOMINANT SEVENTH.

RULE.   *The dominant seventh chord resolves to the tonic triad, to the third of which its seventh must descend.*

NOTE. These rules are for the regular resolution of the dominant seventh chord; later on its irregular resolution will be considered.   (See Lesson 54.)

The resolutions of the intervals in detail are as follows:
The seventh descends to the third of the tonic triad.

The fifth descends parallel with the seventh, to the root of the tonic triad.

Or it may ascend to the third of the tonic triad, in which case the third is doubled, as the seventh is obliged to descend to the same tone.

The third, being the leading tone of the scale, may always ascend to the root of the tonic triad. (Example 42, *a.*) It may also descend in the alto or tenor voices to the fifth of the tonic triad. (Example 42, *d.*)

42.

The root of a dominant seventh chord ascends or descends to the root of the tonic triad, and is often retained as the bass tone of a $\frac{6}{4}$ chord. (See Example 43, *b.*)

When the fifth or third of the dominant seventh chord is omitted, or when the chord appears in any of its inversions, the root is retained in the upper voices. (Example 43, *c.*) In other words, it is often treated as in Lesson I, when it is the bass tone of the dominant triad without the seventh.

The dominant seventh chord is used in three different forms demanded by the exigencies of progression, and while the root and the seventh are always present, the third or fifth may be omitted, and another root substituted in their places. (See Example 46.)

43.

The dominant seventh chord may be repeated in different positions before resolving; this is also true of the principal triads and their inversions. It may be approached in **parallel motion** from a tonic $\frac{6}{4}$ triad, for the reason that the upper voices move only one degree.

44.

NOTE. Parallel motion from any interval to a fifth or octave is to be avoided in outer voices *unless:*

> A connecting tone is present in one of the voices, or
> The other parts move by contrary motion, or
> All the upper voices (as in Example 44) move one degree.

Such progressions are called **concealed** or **hidden** fifths and octaves.

The full figuring of the chord of the dominant seventh is $\frac{7}{5}$, abbreviated to $\frac{7}{5}$ or **7**. In the minor mode the raised leading tone is indicated by a $\sharp$ or $\natural$ under the 7, $\binom{7}{\sharp}$.

The authentic cadence is much strengthened by the addition of the seventh to the dominant chord, and as the forms of the chord with the root doubled all resolve to the complete tonic chord, i.e., without omitted fifth, this chord is perhaps more useful than the complete chord $\frac{7}{5}$. On the other hand the positions with third omitted are of comparatively infrequent use, excepting as passing chords, which are melodic rather than harmonic in character.

This chord now gives us the use of another bass tone in harmonizing the **fourth degree of the scale.** Whereas thus far this degree has only been possible to harmonize as the root of the subdominant, with the root or third in the bass,

45.

6

we can now use it as the **seventh of the dominant** chord — a decided addition to our harmonic vocabulary

THE DOMINANT SEVENTH CHORD IN C MAJOR.

46.

EXERCISES TO LESSON VI.

a. Fifth omitted. *b.* Complete chord.

Play this cadence in every major and minor key.

LESSON VII.

THE FIRST INVERSION OF THE CHORD OF THE DOMINANT SEVENTH.

THE SIX-FIVE DOMINANT CHORD.

In Lesson IV we have used the leading tone in the bass in the chord of the sixth, or first inversion of the dominant triad.

If we now add the original seventh of the dominant chord to this triad, we have the corresponding first inversion of the chord of the dominant seventh which is called the chord of the sixth and fifth or the **six-five chord.**

The full figuring of this chord is $\frac{6}{5}$, abbreviated to $\frac{6}{5}$. In this, as in other inversions of the chord of the dominant seventh, the original **root** is not doubled, nor the fifth omitted. The resolution is the same as in the fundamental position, excepting that the root becomes a connecting tone with the fifth of the tonic triad, and the third (bass tone) always ascends to the root of the same.

The fifth descends to the root of the tonic triad, or ascends, doubling the third of the same.

The seventh descends to the third of the tonic triad.

The root connects with the fifth of the tonic triad as before stated.

By means of these chords we gain the leading tone in the bass in harmonizing the fourth degree of the scale, and we may also utilize it for the fifth and second degrees as before.

EXERCISES TO LESSON VII.

The exercises with given bass should end with a complete cadence when possible.

1. Figured bass given.

2.

3. Unfigured bass.

4. Soprano given.

Harmonize the same in minor.

5.

N.B. Plagal cadence.

6.

Play in every major and minor key.

LESSON VIII.

THE SECOND INVERSION OF THE CHORD OF THE DOMINANT SEVENTH.

THE FOUR-THREE DOMINANT CHORD.

Thus far we have considered no combination which has allowed us the use of the second degree in the bass, except as a passing $\frac{6}{4}$ chord. (See Lesson V.)

By placing the fifth of the dominant seventh chord in the bass, we find a convenient harmony for the fourth, fifth, and seventh degrees of the scale.

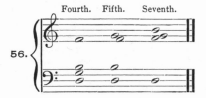

This chord consists of a third, fourth, and sixth, added to the bass tone, and its three positions in close harmony are as follows:

57.

Its full figuring is $\frac{6}{4}\atop{3}$, abbreviated to $\frac{4}{3}$. In the dominant seventh chords of minor keys, the sixth interval is made sharp or natural, to indicate the raised leading tone of the scale.

58.

The resolution is the same as in the fundamental position (Example 59, *a*), with the following notable exception, viz: If the bass tone of the $\frac{4}{3}$ chord ascends, and the original seventh descends, it forms a tonic chord of the sixth with the third doubled (Example 59, *b*). In order to obviate this the seventh may ascend to the fifth of the tonic chord (Example 59, *c*), the parallel fifths which result being excusable from the fact that one of them is not perfect. (Example 59, N.B.)

59.

N. B   This particular form of consecutive fifths is to be found in the works of every great composer from Händel to Brahms. The **real** reason for its legitimacy in this connection lies in the fact that the dominant seventh under these circumstances is a **passing** chord, and therefore melodic.

As in the case of the other positions and inversions of the dominant seventh chord, this may also be exchanged for any inversion of the same chord, or for its fundamental position. Since this chord enables us to utilize the harmonic progression IV–V$_3^4$, we can harmonize the ascending major scale as follows:

This, however, is not possible in the minor mode, on account of the faulty progression of the augmented second between the sixth and seventh degrees.

NOTE. On general principles all progressions of augmented and diminished intervals are to be avoided, *especially* in the inner voices. The very frequent and effective use of augmented seconds and fourths in instrumental compositions in no wise contradicts this principle.

EXERCISES TO LESSON VIII.

3. Unfigured bass.

4. Soprano given.

5.

6.

Play in every major and minor key.

61.

I V4 I6 I IV I6 V I
  3   4

LESSON IX.

THE THIRD INVERSION OF THE CHORD OF THE DOMINANT SEVENTH.

THE FOUR-TWO DOMINANT CHORD.

The third inversion of the dominant seventh chord consists of a second, fourth, and sixth, erected on the fourth degree of the scale. It is called the chord of the $\frac{6}{4}$, often abbreviated to $\frac{4}{2}$ or 2. Its three positions are as follows:

62.

The resolution is to the first inversion of the tonic triad. Its bass tone, being the original seventh of the dominant chord, must descend to the third of the tonic triad, the leading tone progresses as in the fundamental position, and the root forms a connecting tone with the tonic triad.

The fifth, however, has more possible resolutions than in any other position of the dominant seventh chord.

First — It may descend to the root of the tonic triad as above.

Second — It may ascend to the third of the tonic triad, forming a first inversion with the third doubled.

Third — It may ascend or descend to the fifth of the tonic triad. (See Example 65). · The last-named resolution occurs often in dispersed harmony, and will be discussed later. The ascent to the fifth of the tonic triad in the soprano, however, is a very convenient mode of harmonizing the melodic progression, supertonic to dominant, and is found in numberless compositions of the best masters.

As in the other inversions of the dominant seventh, all the intervals must be present, the root not being doubled. Like these, also, the $\frac{4}{2}$ chords may be exchanged for any other inversion of the dominant seventh, but must be eventually resolved. In all cases where the inversions of the dominant seventh are found in an incomplete

form, the chords may be considered as passing chords, or as forms
of melodic progression.

The melodic progression, submediant, leading tone, tonic, is conve-
niently harmonized by the use of the $\frac{4}{2}$ chord, allowing the seventh to
become a connecting tone in the bass with the root of the subdominant chord.

There is one more exception to the general rule for the descent of
the seventh.   It occurs when a fundamental position of the dominant
seventh chord, with the root not doubled, and with the third or fifth
(never with the seventh) in the soprano voice, is followed by the
first inversion of the tonic triad.   In this case — a somewhat rare
one — the seventh ascends to the fifth of the tonic triad, instead of
descending to the third.

The regular resolution of the seventh downward would leave the
tonic triad in a very weak position, and produce concealed octaves,
nearly as objectionable as consecutive octaves.   (See Lesson VI.)

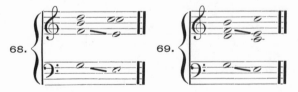

Singular exceptions to the resolution of the $\frac{4}{2}$ chord are found in the
works of Bach.   (Toccata in d minor.)

When the dominant $\frac{4}{2}$ chord occurs in the minor mode the fourth requires a ♮ or ♯, on account of the raised leading tone.

EXERCISES TO LESSON IX.

1. Figured bass given.

2.

3. Unfigured bass.

4. Soprano given.

3 chords.

5.

Play in all major keys.

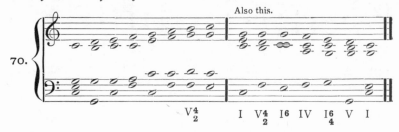

LESSON X.

THE SECONDARY TRIADS IN MAJOR.

THE SUPERTONIC TRIAD.

The secondary triads of the major scale are the minor triads formed
upon its second, third, and sixth degrees. They stand in the relation
of relative minor keys to the principal triads: tonic, subdominant, and
dominant. Their inferiority has caused them to be regarded by many
theorists as entirely subordinate to the principal triads, not as inde-
pendent harmonies, and to be used only as substitutes for, and in connection with, them. If we analyze almost any of the simpler pieces
by Mozart, Beethoven, or Haydn, we shall find that the proportion of
secondary triads is small, and that the fundamental harmonies consist
largely of the tonic, dominant, and subdominant, with modulations to
the adjacent keys. However, the further we go back towards the
contrapuntal era of musical art, the less we find this to be the case,
and even in the works of Bach and Händel they are used with great
independence and freedom.

The most important of these triads is that founded upon the supertonic of the scale, and, being the parallel minor of the subdominant,

its third is often doubled, especially after a tonic chord. Its best usages are as follows:

First — To precede the dominant seventh chord, or tonic $\frac{6}{4}$ triad in a complete cadence, as a substitute for the subdominant.

A skip in the bass from II to I$\frac{6}{4}$ is allowed.

Second — As a passing chord between the tonic triad and its first inversion. (Substitute for the dominant $\frac{6}{4}$.)

Besides these most useful progressions, the following may also be used:

If we utilize the supertonic of the scale as a connecting tone in pro-gressing from the second to the fifth degree we form a succession of two diatonic major thirds.

This progression involves the **false relation of the tritone**, which has been regarded as objectionable in the strictest writing. This is easily avoided by observing the following

RULE. *When the dominant triad (without the seventh) is pre-ceded or succeeded by that of the supertonic, the connecting tone (supertonic) is to be disregarded, and the upper voices are to move in contrary motion to the bass.*

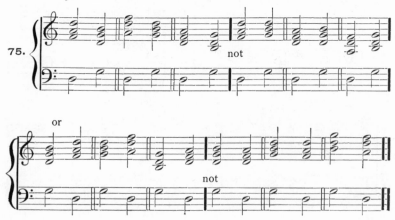

The tritone is the interval of an augmented fourth which exists between the fourth and seventh degrees of the scale. Progressions
which involve these two tones in succession, like

are avoided in strict counterpoint. Example 75, page 34, covers all
necessary progressions of this kind in harmonizing the exercises
given.

EXERCISES TO LESSON X.

a, Third doubled, b. II followed by I$_4^6$.

1. Figured bass given.

2.

3. Unfigured bass.

4. Soprano given.

5.

Play in every major key.

I   I6   IV   II   I6/4   V7   I

LESSON XI.

THE SUBMEDIANT TRIAD.

The secondary triad next in importance is that of the submediant, the parallel of the tonic. It is often used to succeed the dominant or dominant seventh chord instead of the tonic triad, forming what is called the **deceptive cadence.**

In this case the leading tone, if not below the seventh, or in the soprano voice, may descend to the root of the submediant triad. (Example 78, *b*). Otherwise the leading tone generally ascends, in which case the third of the submediant triad is doubled.

This progression (the deceptive cadence) can never take place at the close of a piece.

This chord is also often used as a connecting link between tonic and subdominant triads,

80.

I   VI   IV

but less often between subdominant and tonic.

81.

IV   VI   I

Other possible progressions are as follows:

82.

VI V_7 VI I_4^6 VI I^6

Not good. (See Lesson XII.)   Rare.   Poor.   Possible.   Harsh.

etc.

VI II   VI V_3^4 VI I   VI V_5^6 VI $V2$

All the above progressions must retain the connecting tones in the same voices, or move in contrary motion to the bass. The descending major scales may now be harmonized by means of the submediant chord, in the following manner:

83.
I   V   VI   I   IV   I $\begin{smallmatrix}6\\4\end{smallmatrix}$ V   I

Or much better:

84.

the melodic progression submediant to leading tone having been thus far impossible on account of the succession dominant—subdominant. This may now be combined with the **ascending** major scale (Lesson IX), and must be played in every key from the following model:

1	2	3	4	5	6	7	8	7	6	5	4	3	2	1
I	V	I	IV	I^6	IV	V$\begin{smallmatrix}4\\3\end{smallmatrix}$	I	V	VI	V^6	V$\begin{smallmatrix}6\\5\end{smallmatrix}$	I	V$_7$	I
										or I	IV	I$\begin{smallmatrix}6\\4\end{smallmatrix}$		

EXERCISES TO LESSON XI.

a. Deceptive cadence. b. I VI IV.

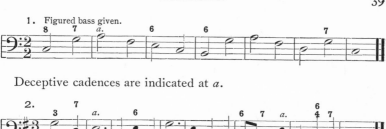

1. Figured bass given.

Deceptive cadences are indicated at *a*.

2.

3. Unfigured bass.

4. Soprano given.

It will be found a useful exercise to set this melody to the words of a hymn.

5.

6.

Play in every key.

85.

I   V₇   VI   IV   I⁶₄   V   I

LESSON XII.

THE MEDIANT TRIAD.

The triad of the mediant, the parallel minor of the dominant, is the least useful of the secondary harmonies of the scale. Its principal use is to harmonize the leading tone, in the descending melodic succession, tonic, leading tone, submediant. This, like the supertonic and submediant triads, is indicated by a small numeral, from the fact that the triad is minor.

Like the submediant, its third is often doubled. It should only be preceded by the tonic or dominant, the progression supertonic to mediant, or subdominant to mediant being harsh in any position.

It may best be succeeded by the subdominant or tonic triad, the succession mediant to submediant, mediant to dominant, or mediant to supertonic being either harsh or weak.

On general principles the progression of a secondary triad to its relative major, supertonic to subdominant, submediant to tonic, or mediant to dominant, although possible, is not to be recommended, although the reverse progression is always of good effect.

The progressions from secondary triads to those a fourth above, although freely used by all modern composers, are avoided in the strictest vocal writing, or else are used in contrary motion, disregarding the connecting tone.

NOTE. The apparently contradictory relation which exists in these successions is due to the fact that these chords appear to be tonics, preceded by **minor** dominants. As all dominant chords are major, these progressions must be false.

Our general rules of progression may now be re-stated, as follows :

First — Move to the nearest position of the succeeding chord.

Second — Use connecting tones with parallel motion.

NOTE. Parallel motion by perfect fifths or octaves is **wrong**. Parallel motion by thirds or sixths is **right**.

Third — Use contrary motion when no connecting tones are present.

NOTE. Also in the succession supertonic to dominant, or its reverse.

Fourth — The third of the supertonic, mediant, and submediant is usually to be doubled.

Fifth — Avoid progressions of augmented and diminished intervals in all voices; also progressions of two fourths or fifths in the same direction in the bass.

With our present chord material the various degrees of the major scale may now be harmonized as follows :

TABLE.

From this table it will be seen that the dominant and the subdominant have a much more varied relationship to the triads of the
scale than the other degrees, being possible to harmonize with every
degree of the scale in the bass except one. The tonic may be harmonized with every degree of the scale except two.

EXERCISES TO LESSON XII.

V III IV   V6V4   III   V6   I6 V V7 I
        5 3   4

1. Figured bass given.

2.

3. Unfigured bass given.

4. Melody given.

5.

Play this cadence in every major key.

I   III   IV   II   I6   V7   I
                 4

91.

LESSON XIII.

INVERSIONS OF THE SECONDARY TRIADS.

The first inversions (chords of the sixth) of the supertonic, mediant, and submediant, are used with almost as much frequency as the fundamental positions, and like them often double the third.

The first inversion of the mediant is of somewhat less value, but has one peculiar usage which is of singularly interesting effect. It consists of the doubling of the third, which, with the root, progresses to the seventh and fifth of the dominant seventh. The effect is that of a double suspension on the dominant seventh, and later on will be so regarded. (Example 92.)

92.

NOTE. The second inversion of the mediant is often used in the same way.

93.

The second inversion of the secondary triads is of very slight value, and its usage is governed by the strictest rules of Lesson V. All $\frac{6}{4}$ chords *sound* like tonic chords, and it is only when their relationship as passing chords is made plainly obvious to the ear, that they can be used in any other way.

94.

As the possible successions of the first inversions of triads require some special treatment they may be summed up as follows:

RULE 1. *A single chord of the sixth doubles the root or fifth* (see Example 95, *a*), *and may double the third in the inversion of the chord of the supertonic, mediant, or submediant.* (See Example 95, *b*.)

RULE 2. *In two successive chords of the sixth, first double the root, or fifth, then the third, or vice versa.*

NOTE. An exception to this is found in the connection of the tonic with the subdominant, if two connecting tones are present.

RULE 3. *In three successive chords of the sixth, with ascending diatonic bass, double the fifth, third, and root in succession.*

Or by Rule 4.

With a descending diatonic bass, double the root, third, and fifth in succession.

RULE 4. *In a succession of sixths where the upper voices all move in contrary motion to the bass, all the thirds may be doubled. This, however, is not often necessary.*

These rules do not apply strictly to dispersed harmony, and are intended to cover only examples in close position.

EXERCISES TO LESSON XIII.

a. Rule 2. *b.* Rule 1. *c.* Rule 3.

N.B. Although this triad has not yet been explained, its usage in this connection is the same as that of the other inversions. See next lesson.

Play in every major key.

LESSON XIV.

THE LEADING TONE TRIAD.

There remains but one more triad of the major scale to be considered, i. e., that of the seventh or leading tone. As the fifth of this chord is a dissonance, being imperfect, it follows that a resolution is required. This we find to be identical with that of the dominant seventh; in fact the triad in itself is a dominant seventh with the root omitted, and is subject to the same treatment as that chord. Its root being a leading tone, is almost never to be doubled (See Example 102, *a*), nor used in the fundamental position, except in sequences.

N.B. This resolution to the tonic triad with doubled third is very common in strict part writing.

Generally it appears as a chord of the sixth, with the third or fifth doubled, and resolves to the tonic triad. In this form it is frequently found in strict writing, in which it forms some cadences of the church modes. (See Example 102, *b*). In modern writing it has been practically superseded by the dominant $\frac{4}{3}$ chord in the authentic cadence.

NOTE. The fundamental position with doubled root appears often in sequences. (See Example 103, *a*, and also Lesson XXXIX.) Its use in the second inversion is also very infrequent, but it is occasionally used in the place of a dominant $\frac{4}{2}$ chord, in the same manner as any other $\frac{6}{4}$ chord. (See Example 103, *b*.)

This triad is utilized as follows in harmonizing the major scale:

EXERCISES TO LESSON XIV

1. Figured bass given.

Sequence.

2.

3. Unfigured bass.

4. Melody given.

5.

Play in every major key. Also all the major scales with the harmony given in Example 104.

105.

I VII⁰6 I6 IV I6 V I
4 7

LESSON XV.

THE SECONDARY TRIADS IN MINOR, WITH THEIR INVERSIONS.

The secondary triads in the minor mode are treated similarly to those of the major. Being formed from the tones of the minor scale, they all contain discords except the submediant, which is a major triad.

The **supertonic** is a diminished triad, corresponding to the leading tone triad of the relative major.

$c:$ II° equivalent to
$E\flat:$ VII°

The **mediant** is an augmented triad, consisting of a major third and augmented fifth. The augmentation of the fifth is indicated by the sign + (III $^+$).

107.

This chord is not used for the present for harmonizing purposes, but will be considered later on under chromatic passing tones.

The **submediant** is a major triad, the parallel of the subdominant.

NOTE. The root of the submediant in major is frequently doubled, but in minor never if preceded or succeeded by the dominant.

108.

The **leading tone** triad is also diminished, and coincides with the leading tone of the tonic major triad, being in fact the third, fifth, and seventh of a dominant seventh chord. Both diminished triads are more frequently used in their first inversions, usually with the third or fifth doubled, than in the fundamental position.

109.   etc.

The root of the supertonic triad is more frequently doubled, however, than that of the leading tone.   The rules for the use of these
chords are the same as in Lessons X, XI, XII, and XIII.

EXERCISES TO LESSON XV.

3. Unfigured bass.

4. Melody given.

5.

LESSON XVI.

SUMMARY.

We have now considered all the triads that it is possible to erect upon the various degrees of the major and minor scales, with their first and second inversions. The following table gives a summarized view of these triads in the key of F major and minor. The term *rare* is of course to be understood in a comparative sense.

TABLE I.

TABLE OF TRIADS OF THE MAJOR AND MINOR SCALES, WITH THEIR FIRST AND SECOND INVERSIONS.

In F major.

It will be observed that all the above $\frac{6}{4}$ chords are to be used in strict accordance with the rules of Lesson V.

This table is to be played at the instrument in every major and minor key, from the Roman numerals.

The next table presents the available progression of each triad to the other triads of the scale.

TABLE II.

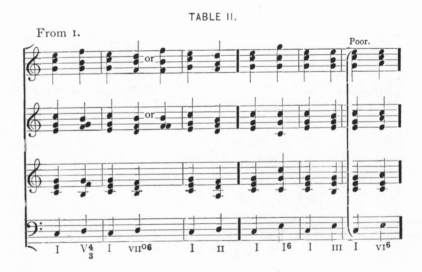

From vii°(only in sequences).

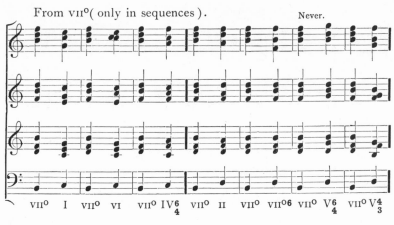

Poor.   Rare.

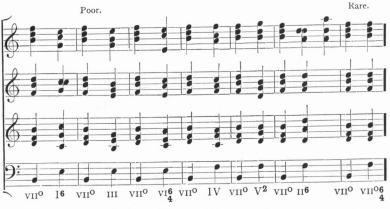

Poor.   Bad.

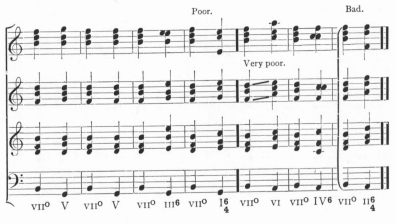

It is *indispensable* that the student should have both of these tables at his finger ends as well as in his head, in every major and minor key. They form in themselves alone a fundamental system of diatonic harmony which, if thoroughly mastered, will be of the greatest assistance in all future studies. Although these tables do not give the possible progression between inversions of chords, these are sufficiently controlled by the principles heretofore given.

This second table remains the same in the minor mode, omitting all progressions **to** and **from** the mediant triad (III$^+$). Like the major, it should be played in every key.

After a careful study of these tables it may be well to omit the progressions to all the $\frac{6}{4}$ chords, excepting those of the tonic. The examples marked "rare," "poor," and "never" (always comparative terms) are improved by the use of *other* chords in harmonizing the soprano.

LESSON XVII.

DISPERSED HARMONY. (Open Position.)

If the three upper voices of a chord, soprano, alto, and tenor, lie outside the compass of one octave, the harmony is usually said to be dispersed, or in open position.* (See Introduction.) This does not alter the original doubling of the intervals, however; that is to say, when the root, third, or fifth is doubled in close position, it is also doubled in the corresponding position in open harmony. In short the difference between the two positions consists only in the inversion of the alto and tenor voices.

110.

From this it will be seen that the tenor of the close, becomes the alto of the open position. The alto being inverted into the lower octave forms the tenor, and vice versa.

* There are some exceptions to this definition. It is given as the most practical general rule.

The following table shows triad and seventh chords in every position and inversion, in close and open harmony.

TABLE.

The open positions of the above chords are to be played in every key.

The preference between close and open harmony in vocal music is decided by the compass of the voices. For instance:

111.

This is equally favorable and practicable in both positions of the chord, as all the voices lie well within their own compass.

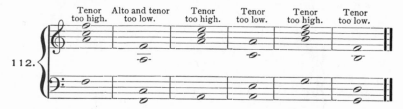

But this leads the tenor too high in close position, and, on the other hand, too low in open position. Well written four part harmony contains both open and close positions, according to the compass and effect of the voices, but it is safe to harmonize any soprano above

in open, and below that tone in close position.

Exceptions may be made for special effects, but these may be safely deferred to a later period. It is by no means to be understood, however, that the inner voices are to skip from open to close position and vice versa whenever the soprano voice moves above or

below The change from one to the other is always combined with a smooth progression of the alto and tenor.

It often happens that, in the case of a wide leap in the soprano or bass, the thirds and fifths of the principal triads are doubled temporarily.

The tenor may, if necessary, lie more than an octave above the bass, but the soprano and alto, or alto and tenor, should not move more than an octave apart.

The following position, however, is often found, *especially for instruments*, and is of very good effect.

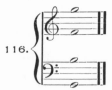

The major scale may now be harmonized in open and close position as follows:

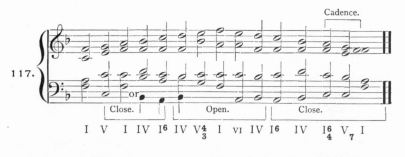

The major scale in the bass may be harmonized as follows:

EXERCISES TO LESSON XVII.

1. Figured bass given.

3. Unfigured bass given.

4. Melody given.

5.

All the major scales are now to be harmonized at the pianoforte, in the soprano and bass voices, according to the models given above. These cadences are also to be transposed into every major key.

119.

LESSON XVIII.

DISPERSED HARMONY (Open Position) IN MINOR.

The exercises for harmonizing in the open position in minor keys present no new difficulties. The interval of the augmented second between the sixth and seventh degrees, although much used in all forms of instrumental composition, is much better avoided, especially in the alto and tenor voices.

120.

As a purely melodic interval it often has rare expressiveness.

121.

Harmonize the harmonic minor scale in every key, ascending and descending, according to the following model :

122.

Review all previous work. *Play all the exercises from the given soprano and bass, and transpose them, up and down, a half and whole step.* It will also be found useful to play the exercises of the first fifteen lessons in dispersed harmony. The student may also compose such exercises for himself, according to the given models.

EXERCISE TO LESSON XVIII.

Play in all minor keys.

LESSON XIX.

THE DOMINANT NINTH IN MAJOR, AND ITS INVERSIONS.

The chord of the dominant ninth is formed by adding a third to the seventh in its highest voice. In four-voiced harmony the original fifth is often omitted, the third and seventh never. The ninth of this chord (the third above the seventh) must not appear less than nine degrees above the root. Such positions as

are therefore inadmissible. This chord being a dominant harmony like the dominant seventh, its resolution is to the tonic chord, the ninth descending parallel to the seventh. In this case the bass is sometimes connected with the fifth of the tonic, forming a tonic $\frac{6}{4}$ chord.

If the fifth is present in the chord, and lies **below** the ninth, it must ascend to the third of the tonic, to avoid the consecutive fifths which would result from parallel motion with the ninth.

Sometimes the ninth resolves before the rest of the chord, forming a dominant seventh, which is then resolved.

This, however, can hardly be considered as a true chord of the ninth, being simply a dislocation of the root of the dominant seventh. This will be considered later under the subject of **Suspensions.** (See Lesson LV.) The first and third inversions of this chord are the most practicable in four-part harmony, although the second may be used if the ninth lies in the upper voice. The fourth inversion is not used for the reasons before stated. (Example 124.)

In the exercises of this lesson the ninth appears only in the soprano
and tenor voices. The following resolution has been used by some
modern composers:

129.

The major ninth is useful in harmonizing the major scale descending, as it facilitates the progression from the seventh to the sixth
degree.

130.

I   V   V   I   IV   I⁶₄   V₇   I
          9

Play all the major scales with this harmony.

The ninth is best introduced as a connecting tone with the preceding chord, or as a diatonic tone from the next degree above or below.
It may also be introduced by a skip from the third, fifth, or seventh
of the dominant, and may change position by repetition, like any of
the preceding chords.

EXERCISES TO LESSON XIX.

a. Ninth prepared.

1. Figured bass given.

2. Melody given.

Play in every major key.

LESSON XX.

THE DOMINANT NINTH IN MINOR.

The treatment of the dominant ninth in minor does not differ from that of the major, excepting that the ninth may be placed in any voice except the bass. The fifth is omitted in four part writing, and the ninth, as in the major mode, must never appear less than nine degrees above the root.

etc.

* Seventh in the bass.

Like the dominant major ninth, this chord may be introduced by diatonic progression, by preparation, or by skips from any tone of the dominant seventh. Skips of an augmented second or augmented fourth are, however, to be avoided. It may change places by repetition with any of the tones of the dominant seventh, without skipping an augmented fourth or second, but must be strictly resolved.

133.

As in the case of the dominant major ninth, the fifth, if present, must ascend when it lies below the ninth. (See Example 134, *a*.) It may, however, as often found in the works of Bach, descend to the fifth of the tonic triad, thus:

134.

The inversions with the third and seventh in the bass are the most useful.

EXERCISES TO LESSON XX.

1. Melody given.

4. CHANT.

5.

*Seventh in the Bass.

Play in all minor keys.

135.

LESSON XXI.

THE CHORD OF THE SEVENTH ON THE LEADING TONE.

If we erect a chord of the seventh on the seventh degree of a major key, we shall find that its tones are identical with those of the dominant ninth chord considered in the preceding lessons, in fact such chords, from the fact that their tones find a common generator in the dominant, are practically dominant ninth chords with their roots omitted. They are in every respect so introduced and resolved. The positions and inversions of the leading tone seventh in major are as follows:

It will be seen that in all positions in which the third, originally the fifth of the dominant ninth, appears below the seventh, it ascends, doubling the third of the tonic triad. Parallel fifths would result from the fifth descending to the tonic, (see Example 137) therefore

RULE 1. *The third, when below the seventh, must ascend to the third of the tonic, doubling its third. Otherwise it may ascend or descend.*

NOTE. This is of course the same rule which applies to the **fifth** of the dominant ninth chord in the preceding lesson.

137.

Rule 2. *No intervals of this chord are doubled or omitted.*

138.

Note. The third of this chord is sometimes resolved upward or downward to the fifth of the tonic, in order to avoid doubling its third (see Lessons XIX and XX), but this usage is not to be recommended for the present. At best it exchanges a very audible concealed fifth for the doubled third.

139.

Otherwise the treatment of this chord and its inversions is identical with that of the dominant major ninth.

EXERCISES TO LESSON XXI.

Play in all major keys.

LESSON XXII.

THE CHORD OF THE DIMINISHED SEVENTH.

The chord of the diminished seventh so-called, or the dominant minor ninth, without its root (vii^9_{70}) is one of the most useful and valuable combinations with which we have to deal. Although having no existence, fundamentally speaking, in the major mode, it is yet freely introduced in that mode by flatting the minor seventh melodically.

141.

It consists of a combination of three minor thirds, and contains no perfect consonance between the intervals of any position or inversion. It may therefore be approached by parallel motion with impunity.

142.

Its three positions with resolution in the key of c minor are as follows:

143.

At a the third ascends to the third of the tonic, as in the corresponding chord in the major mode. The **descent** to the fifth of the tonic is also occasionally used. The augmented second between the sixth and seventh degrees is to be avoided in the inner voices. The rules for the introduction and resolution of the diminished seventh are the same as given in the preceding lesson.

EXERCISES TO LESSON XXII.

Play in every minor key.

LESSON XXIII.

THE INVERSIONS OF THE DIMINISHED SEVENTH.

The three inversions of the din.inished seventh are used with as much freedom as the fundamental position. The peculiarities of the resolution of each inversion are as follows:

First — Since the third, in the first inversion, is in the bass, and therefore necessarily below the seventh, it must ascend to the third of the tonic triad, forming a chord of the sixth with the **third** doubled. (Example 145, *a.*)

145.

Sometimes, however, the fifth also ascends, forming a chord of the sixth with the **fifth** doubled. (Example 145, *b.*) This only happens when it is below the root, otherwise consecutive fifths result. (Example 145, *c.*)

Second — The fifth of the chord, when in the bass, may descend, forming a chord of the sixth with the third or root doubled (Example 146, *a*), or ascend to the fifth of the tonic, forming a $\frac{6}{4}$ chord. (Example 146, *b.*)

146.

The first resolution given at *b* is bad on account of the progression of the two fourths in the outer voices. An exceptional progression of the $\text{VII}^{o\frac{4}{3}}$ is seen at Example 146, *c*, in which the first fifth is imperfect. It is not recommended, however. The second is much better.

Third — Since the seventh descends to the fifth of the tonic triad, when in the bass it must form a $\frac{6}{4}$ chord with the root or third doubled.

147.
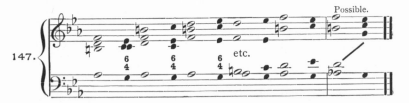

As in all preceding lessons, the different positions of all these inversions may be exchanged for one another before resolving, avoiding, however, all progressions of augmented seconds, augmented fourths, diminished thirds, etc.

Play all the inversions of the diminished seventh chord in every minor key.

EXERCISES TO LESSON XXIII.

The I_4^6 chord in the cadence may be approached by the VII^{o4}_3 or $_2^4$ instead of by the subdominant chord, viz :

Play in every key.

LESSON XXIV.

THE CHORD OF THE DIMINISHED SEVENTH. (Continued.)

As before stated the diminished seventh chord is freely used in the major mode as a melodic alteration, and since it only differs from the dominant seventh by one semitone, as a matter of scale degrees, it follows that the second, fourth, and seventh, which are common to both, may be harmonized as well by one as

* Changes of position are indicated by the order of the figures.

the other. In case of change of position by repetition, the figures
indicate the intervals in the upper voice.

EXERCISES TO LESSON XXIV.

LESSON XXV.

MODULATION.

The connection of chords belonging to different keys by means of harmonies common to both is called **modulation.** As different keys are said to be **related,** in proportion to the number of tones in common between them, it follows that those of the dominant and sub-dominant, with their parallels, are the nearest in tonality to any given tonic. For instance:

Scale of C — C D E F G A B C.
Scale of G —   G A B C D E F♯ G.
Scale of F —   F G A B♭ C D E F.

Every tone of G major exists in C major except F♯.
Every tone of F major exists in C major except B♭.

These chords as **tonics** coincide with the triads erected on the II, III, IV, V, and VI degrees of the scale, and when a simple melody forsakes its own key temporarily, it usually does not stray further away than to one of these related keys.

NOTE. Some theorists define related keys as those whose signatures differ by not more than one accidental.

The mere succession of chords of different keys does not necessarily constitute a modulation. In fact, it is entirely possible for any two major tonic chords to succeed one another in such a manner as to be mutually related to the same key. For example:

149.

The tonic triad of C major and the tonic triad of D♭ major are also the dominant and submediant of the key of *f* minor. (Example 149, *a.*)

The tonic triad of C major and the tonic triad of B major are also the submediant and dominant of the key of *e* minor. (Example 149, *b.*)

All the other possible successions of major tonic triads will be found demonstrated in Lesson LII.

A change of tonality convincing to the ear must be accomplished by means of a connecting harmony which contains a tone or tones foreign to the original key and belonging to the new one.

The chords most commonly used for this purpose are the **dominant** and **diminished seventh,** and for this reason: The major and minor triads and seventh chords on every degree of the scale excepting the fifth and seventh (seventh of minor only) are ambiguous in tonality, being related to more than one key.

150.

Such triads are supertonics, mediants, dominants, subdominants, and submediants, according to their relation to a given tonic. The combination of major triad and minor seventh (V_7), or diminished triad with diminished seventh (vii^o_{7o}), however, is never found except on the dominant of the major and minor, and on the seventh of the minor, respectively. (See Example 150, *a.*)

151.

C :I   V C : 1 G : V_7 I

If now the progression at *a* is given the ear recognizes the G triad as the dominant of the key of C. But if we interpose the chord x in Example *b*, the G triad becomes a new tonic preceded by its dominant.

If, then, the change of key is to be made permanent, the modulation must be followed by a complete cadence in the new key, in any of the forms which reiterate its fundamental harmonies.

A formula for a permanent change of key might therefore be as follows :

Let *x* represent the key to be modulated into.

Let *a* represent the key to be modulated from.

Original key.	Modulating chord and resolution.	Cadence in new key.
$a : I$	$x :$ vii $^9_{7o}$ or V_7 I	IV I^6_4 V I

Since any given tonic may be succeeded by the dominant or diminished seventh of any other key (in one way or another), it follows that the above formula stands for a complete system of modulation from any key to all the others.

For this lesson, however, we will confine our work to the modulation from tonic to dominant, using both the dominant and diminished sevenths as modulating chords.

152.

$C : I$ G :V_7 I

At *a*, *b*, *c*, and *d* the root of the tonic chord of C major becomes the seventh of the dominant chord of G. Any inversion of the dominant seventh may be used.

At *e*, *f*, and *g* the root of the tonic chord of C major becomes the fifth of the chord on the seventh degree (diminished seventh chord) in the key of G. The position at *h* is not possible on account of the false relation E–E♭ between the bass and alto.

NOTE. The false relation, or unharmonic cross relation, is a contradictory succession of harmony. It consists in progressing to any tone which is chromatically altered, when that tone is preceded, in some other voice, by its octave *without* the chromatic alteration.

The following tables give the modulation from the tonic to the dominant of C major, with every position and inversion of the V_7 and VII°_7 chords.

TABLE I.

MODULATIONS TO THE DOMINANT, WITH THE V^7.

TABLE II.

MODULATION TO THE DOMINANT, WITH VII$\frac{O}{70}$.

NOTE. As before explained, the diminished seventh belongs strictly to the minor mode only, but its use as a melodic form in major is so common and familiar, even in the most unpretentious compositions, and its usefulness so great as a medium for modulation, that the student may well become familiar with it at this point.

All the other positions of this modulation should also be thoroughly learned in every key at the pianoforte.

LESSON XXVI.

THE MODULATION TO THE SUBDOMINANT.

The subdominant (or dominant below the tonic) is as nearly related (as a key) to the tonic as is the dominant **above** the tonic. In modulating to this key through its dominant seventh, the root, third, and fifth of the tonic become the root, third, and fifth of the dominant seventh in the new key, the minor seventh being merely added to the chord.

155.

C:I F:V₇ I

In the modulation through the diminished seventh the position at *a* is bad on account of the augmented second in the tenor.

156.

C : I F: VII $^0_{70}$

This may be avoided by approaching the seventh from the root of the tonic as at *b*, *c*, and *d*, whereby the third of *C*: I becomes the root of *F*: VII$^0_{70}$, and the fifth of *C*: I becomes the third of *F*: VII$^0_{70}$.

Transpose into all keys.

I F:V₇ I

$$I \quad F{:}\text{vii}^{o}_{70} \quad I \qquad II$$

The following tables give the modulation from the tonic to the subdominant of C major, with every position and inversion of the V_7 and vii^{o}_{70} chords.

TABLE I.

MODULATION TO THE IV, WITH V_7 CHORD.

* Undesirable position.

TABLE II.

WITH THE VII $\frac{o}{7o}$ CHORD.

* Undesirable position.

EXERCISES TO LESSON XXVI.

LESSON XXVII.

FORM OF MODULATION BETWEEN THE TONIC, DOMINANT, AND SUBDOMINANT CHORDS.

The two modulations, from tonic to dominant and from dominant to tonic, may now be combined, forming a temporary modulation from the tonic to dominant and return, or from the tonic to the subdominant and return, since the relation of tonic to subdominant is the same as that of dominant to tonic, and that of tonic to dominant the

* Undesirable position.

same as that of subdominant to tonic.   Such a combination would be
as follows :

157.

$C:$ I $G:$V I $C:$V   I   IV   I   V   I $C:$ I $F:$V$_7$ I $C:$V$_7$ I   IV   I   V$_7$ I

Play in every major and minor key, using this formula.

EXERCISES TO LESSON XXVII.

1. Soprano given.   2.

$G:$V$_7$ I $C:$V$_7$ $E^b:$V$_7$

$B^b:$V$_7$ $B^b:$V$_7$ $E^b:$V$_7$

4.

CHANT.

LESSON XXVIII.

MODULATION FROM A MAJOR KEY TO ITS PARALLEL MINOR.

In modulating from a given major key to its parallel minor through the dominant seventh the third of the original tonic triad becomes the root of the new dominant seventh chord.

This connecting tone is not utilized in case the **complete** dominant seventh is used in the fundamental position.

The progression from the original tonic to the diminished seventh of the new key may be by either contrary or parallel motion. (See Lesson XXII.)

The bass progression to the root of the diminished seventh at *a* is not to be recommended, as it involves either an augmented fifth or a

diminished fourth. This is also true when the first inversion of the
dominant seventh (V_5^6) is used.

161.

Both of these progressions may be disguised by using the modulating tone as a chromatic passing tone from the root of the original
dominant.

162.

This properly belongs to the subject of chromatic alterations,
however, which will be considered later.

The available positions of this modulation are here given:

TABLE.

With third inversion.

With vii^o₇o.

* Weak position.

This table is to be transposed into every key at the pianoforte.

EXERCISES TO LESSON XXVIII.

Either the dominant or diminished seventh may be used as a modulating chord.

I IV   I

LESSON XXIX.

MODULATION FROM A MINOR KEY TO ITS PARALLEL MAJOR.

The modulation from a given minor key to its parallel major by means of the dominant seventh involves progression by contrary motion. The different positions are as follows:

TABLE I.

(*a.*) With the V 7.

If the third of the dominant seventh chord in the fundamental position ascends while the fifth descends, a tonic chord with three roots is formed, which is not a strong position. (See Table I, *a*, 1, 4, 5.) This is avoided (see Table I, *a*, 2, 3, 6) by allowing the leading tone to **descend** — not being in the upper voice.

The consecutive fifths at *a*, 2, 3, and *b*, 1, 4, 5, and 6, etc., are correct on account of the second one being imperfect, and of the contrary motion in the bass, and above all from the fact that they are in the inner voices.

Inversely the consecutive fifths at *b*, 2 and 3 are to be avoided for the same reason, even though the second one is imperfect.

The third inversion of the dominant seventh (V^4_2) is not useful in this modulation on account of the rough skip to the seventh in the bass.

In all the other positions the seventh enters diatonically.

The positions of the diminished seventh chord in this modulation are as follows:

TABLE II.

* Weak position.

The consecutive fifths at *d*, 2 and 3 are to be avoided for the same reason as at *b*, 2 and 3.

The third inversion of the diminished seventh (vii^{o4}_{2}) resolves to the tonic $\frac{6}{4}$ chord with the third doubled (see Example *g*, 1, 3, 6), or with the root doubled (*g*, 2, 4, 5).

These two tables are to be transposed into all keys.

EXERCISES TO LESSON XXIX.

LESSON XXX.

PRACTICAL MODULATIONS RESULTING FROM THE PRECEDING LESSON.

The modulations mentioned in Lessons XXVIII and XXIX may now be combined, forming a modulating phrase in major, thus: I: modulation to vi: modulation to I and cadence. Or in minor, thus: 1: modulation to III: modulation to 1 and cadence. In other words, from a major tonic to its parallel minor and return, or from a

minor tonic to its parallel major and return. Such modulating
phrases might be as follows:

Harmonize the following melodies in like manner.

EXERCISES TO LESSON XXX.

LESSON XXXI.

MODULATION FROM A MAJOR KEY TO THE PARALLEL MINOR OF ITS DOMINANT.

This modulation presents a slight difficulty in the progression from the original tonic to the dominant seventh chord, i.e., if the bass progresses from the root of the one to that of the other, it compels either an augmented second or consecutive octave in some other voice;

165.

therefore

RULE. *When the root of the tonic triad in the bass progresses to the root of the modulating dominant seventh, double the third of the tonic* (see Table I, 1, 2, 3, 4, 5, 6), *or in other words, approach the third of the dominant seventh from the third of the tonic, never from the root. Consecutive fifths also result from parallel motion of the root and fifth of the tonic to the root and fifth of the dominant seventh,* **when the fifth is above the root.**

166.

For this reason, as well as on account of the abrupt skip to the dissonance of the seventh (as in Lesson XXIX), it is better not to use the third inversion in this modulation.

The available positions of this modulation through the dominant seventh are as follows:

TABLE I.

At *c* an inversion of the intervals in the bass, while not forbidden, would be much less melodious.

The modulation through the diminished seventh chord is somewhat smoother than that through the dominant seventh, on account of the root of the original tonic becoming the seventh of the modulating chord. The free upward progression of the third at Table II, *f*, 3, 4, 6, is particularly strong. The positions are as follows:

TABLE II.

Transpose into every key.

EXERCISES TO LESSON XXXI.

LESSON XXXII.

MODULATION FROM A MINOR KEY TO THE SUBDOMINANT OF ITS PARALLEL MAJOR.

This smooth change of key (the reverse of the preceding one) presents no difficulty, as two tones are common between the tonic triad and the dominant seventh, and one between the tonic triad and the diminished seventh.

The third and fifth of the original tonic triad become the root and third of the new dominant seventh, and the fifth of the original tonic triad becomes the root of the diminished seventh.   The positions and inversions, all of which are entirely practicable, are as follows:

TABLE I.

The positions and inversions with the diminished seventh are as follows:

TABLE II.

The weak positions of the tonic triad in Table II, *a*, 1 and 2, *b*, 1, *c*, 1, etc., are caused by the necessary ascent of the third of the chord of the diminished seventh which lies below the seventh. This is avoided by the free leading at *c*, 5 and 6.

The **third** inversion of the chord of the diminished seventh is not practicable in this modulation, as it involves the very unmelodious bass progression of a **diminished fourth** upward, or an **augmented fifth** downward. No interval is perhaps more difficult for the singer.

167.

EXERCISES TO LESSON XXXII.

LESSON XXXIII.

MODULATION FROM A MINOR KEY TO THE SUBDOMINANT OF ITS PARALLEL MAJOR. (Continued.)

The combination of the two modulations given in Lessons XXXI and XXXII gives us the successions: with major tonic, I: modulation to III: modulation to I; with minor tonic, I: modulation to VI: modulation to I.

Such a modulating phrase with a plagal cadence might be as follows:

And with an authentic cadence :

Harmonize the following exercises in like manner, using either dominant or diminished sevenths with their inversions.

EXERCISES TO LESSON XXXIII.

LESSON XXXIV.

MODULATION FROM A MAJOR KEY TO THE PARALLEL MINOR OF ITS SUBDOMINANT.

When the dominant seventh is used to effect this change of key the third of the tonic triad becomes the fifth of the dominant seventh chord, the fifth of the tonic triad becomes the seventh of the dominant seventh chord, and the root is raised a semitone to become the third of the dominant seventh chord, and in order to avoid a false relation this must also take place in whichever voice it originally exists. It is for this reason that *b*, 5 and 6, is to be avoided. (See Table I.)

NOTE. To be sure, this example is not strictly a false relation, but it has the effect of one on account of the skip in the soprano voice.

When the diminished seventh chord is used the third and fifth of the tonic triad remain the third and fifth of the diminished seventh chord. One root (when doubled), is raised to become the root of the diminished seventh chord, while the other descends a whole tone, becoming the diminished seventh of the chord: or the seventh may enter freely if all the parts move in parallel motion, as stated in Lesson XXII. The consecutive fifths in Example 169, *a*, are quite correct.

169.

The third is doubled in the resolution of the seventh chord, and sometimes the root. (See Table II.) Transpose these tables into all keys at the pianoforte.

TABLE I.

a, 1. Dominant seventh chord, either complete or incomplete.

b, 5 and 6. See note, page 110.

c, 3. The only way to raise the root in the same voice.

d, 1. The second progression is the better. The skip to the seventh in the bass is excused by the lack of motion in other parts.

TABLE II.

a, 1 and 2. Doubles either root or third.

a, 4–6. Doubles the third.

b, 6. The fifth, being below the root, may ascend.

c, 2. The second progression is useful.

c, 5. The consecutive fifths are allowed in the inner voices.

d, 4. The free ascent of the third avoids a poor position of the new tonic.

All the other positions at *d* are weak, but unavoidable.

The exercises to be harmonized contain no other positions than those given. Either the V$_7$ or vii$^o_7$ may be used.

EXERCISES TO LESSON XXXIV.

The last exercise may be written freely for the pianoforte with parts doubled.

LESSON XXXV.

MODULATION FROM A MINOR KEY TO THE DOMINANT OF ITS PARALLEL MAJOR.

This modulation is the reverse of the preceding one. In connecting the tonic triad with the new dominant seventh, the root and third of the tonic triad become the fifth and seventh of the dominant seventh chord. (See Table I.)

In connecting the tonic triad with the new diminished seventh chord, the root and third of the tonic triad become the third and fifth of the diminished seventh chord, and the fifth is chromatically lowered, becoming the diminished seventh of the modulating chord. As in the preceding lesson, this must take place in the same voice in which the fifth is already present. (See Table II.)

TABLE I.

The inversions *b* and *c* are somewhat smoother than the fundamental position at *a*.

At *d*, 3 and 5, the connecting tone is disregarded in order to avoid

which is less audible when distributed as at *d*, 4.

TABLE II.

The skip to the diminished seventh in the bass at *d*, 2, is excused by the smoothness of the other voices. At *d*, 2, the free ascent of the third completes the chord. At *d*, 4, the crossing of the tenor by the bass compels the change of position.

EXERCISES TO LESSON XXXV.

LESSON XXXVI.

COMBINATION OF THE PRECEDING MODULATIONS.

The exercises of Lessons XXXIV and XXXV may be combined, forming complete periods containing a modulation from a major key to its supertonic and return, or from a minor key to its minor seventh degree and return.

171.

The others may be combined in the same way.

Our modulating phrases may be made more artistic by the use of the **deceptive cadence** (the triad of the submediant following the dominant seventh chord), since the chord of the subdominant in the final cadence may succeed the submediant as well as the tonic.

$$a : I \; xV_7 \; vi \text{ or } vi \; IV \; I_4^6 \; V \; I$$

x stands for the new key.

This formula, applied to some of the given modulations, gives

I to V.   I to IV.   I to VI.

G : VI   F : V₇   a : V₇

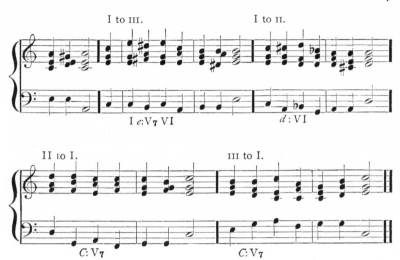

By combining all the modulations already given, as temporary transitions from key to key, an interesting harmonic fabric is formed, which may be illustrated thus:

Write such passages through the following keys, ending with a perfect cadence.

1. D – b – G – e – D – G – D.
2. a – d – F – B♭ – g – d – a.
3. B♭ – F – g – D – g – F – B♭.
4. e – C – a – G – C – e.
5. F – g – B♭ – E♭ – c – F – B♭ – F.

LESSON XXXVII.

THE SUPERTONIC SEVENTH IN MAJOR AND MINOR.

The chords of the seventh formed by adding a third to the upper interval of the secondary triads of the scale are much more restricted in their use than the primary discords, the dominant seventh and ninth.

Of these the seventh chord upon the supertonic is the most important in both major and minor, being often used to precede the dominant or tonic triad in the complete cadence; in fact, it is utilized in practically the same manner as the supertonic triad (see Lesson X), and, being a combination of the tones of the subdominant and supertonic, is of great effect in strengthening the cadence. The seventh of the chord, which may appear in any voice, should be introduced:

First, as a connecting tone with the tonic:

Second, as a descending passing tone between the second and seventh degrees of the scale:

This principle applies to the other secondary seventh chords as well.

RULE.   *Sevenths of secondary chords should be introduced as connecting or descending passing tones.*

NOTE. This of course does not deprive the seventh of its right to enter from another interval of the *same* chord.

The supertonic seventh chord has two resolutions.

First, to the dominant chord, with or without the seventh (see Table I), in which the seventh (of the supertonic chord) descends one degree.

This resolution is perhaps the more frequent when the seventh enters as a passing tone.

Second, to the tonic chord or one of its inversions, in which case the seventh of the chord remains stationary. (See Table II.)

The resolutions are here given in every position.

TABLE I.

RESOLUTION TO THE DOMINANT.

a.   The fifth of the dominant seventh chord is omitted; or it might be connected in the bass, forming a V_3^4 chord.

b.   Perhaps the strongest of the three inversions.

The resolution to V_2^4 is much the better.

TABLE II.

RESOLUTION TO THE TONIC.

(d.)

a, b. The resolution to the I^6 with the third doubled is not to be recommended.

c. Here the resolution to the I^6 is still weaker on account of the skip in the bass.

d. The use of this position may well be deferred to a later period.

These positions and resolutions are the same in the minor mode.

EXERCISES TO LESSON XXXVII.

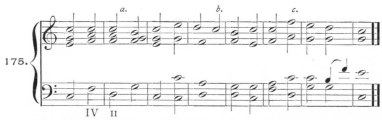

175.

a. Seventh prepared from IV.

b. Seventh enters as a passing tone.

e. Seventh enters from another interval of the same chord.

Play Tables I and II, *a*, in every major and minor key.

LESSON XXXVIII.

INVERSIONS OF THE SUPERTONIC SEVENTH CHORD.

The inversions of the supertonic seventh chord present no new difficulties. The introduction and resolution of the intervals is the same as in the fundamental position, and is alike in both major and minor.

EXERCISES TO LESSON XXXVIII.

Play Tablés I and II, *b*, *c*, *d*, in every major and minor key.

LESSON XXXIX.

SECONDARY SEVENTH CHORDS OF THE TONIC, MEDIANT, SUBDOMINANT, AND SUBMEDIANT, IN MAJOR.

The chords of the seventh on the tonic, mediant, subdominant, and submediant are practically dislocations (suspensions and passing chords) of the other chords of the scale, and are treated as such. The sevenths of the tonic and subdominant, being major, often resolve upward when prepared by a connection with the preceding chord. On the other hand the sevenths of the mediant and submediant, which are minor, usually descend one degree. (See Table.) The fifth of these chords is often omitted, especially when they succeed one another in sequences, which is not seldom the case. When the bass progresses by fourths and fifths, the third of one chord becomes the seventh of the next, and the fifth is omitted in alternate chords.

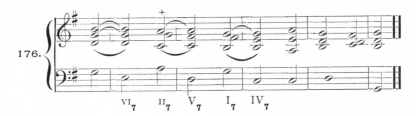

176.

VI_7 II_7 V_7 I_7 IV_7

The following Table shows the common resolutions of these chords in C major.

TABLE.

(a.) The I_7

II^6

The III_7

(b.) The IV_7

The VI₇

a. The I$_7$ resolves to either the I, II, or IV.

b. The IV$_7$ resolves to either the IV, V, II, or VII°(in sequence only).

EXERCISES TO LESSON XXXIX.

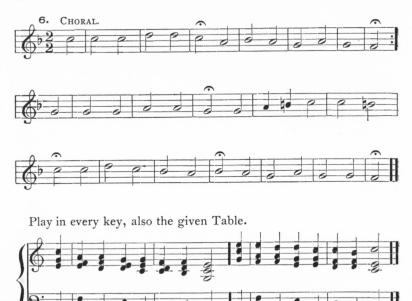

Play in every key, also the given Table.

LESSON XL.

SECONDARY SEVENTH CHORDS IN MINOR.

The remaining dissonant chords of our harmonic system, founded upon the tonic, mediant, subdominant, and submediant of the minor mode, require but little explanation.

The tonic seventh chord consists of a **minor triad** with a **major** seventh.

The mediant seventh chord consists of an **augmented triad** with a **major** seventh.

The subdominant seventh chord consists of a **minor triad** with a **minor** seventh.

The submediant seventh chord consists of a **major triad** with a **major** seventh.

The major seventh of the tonic and the augmented fifth of the mediant chord, being the leading tone of the scale, must ascend to the tonic. (See Example 177, *a*.)

NOTE. In this connection it may be remarked that the seventh of the descending **melodic** minor scale is often used in these chords instead of the leading tone, both chords being indicated by I7, and III7. (See Example 178, *b, c*.)

The other seventh chords are used in the same manner as those of the preceding lesson.

EXERCISES TO LESSON XL.

LESSON XLI.

INVERSIONS OF THE SECONDARY SEVENTH CHORDS IN MAJOR AND MINOR.

The inversions of the secondary seventh chords, in both major and minor, are introduced and resolved in the same manner as the fundamental positions, and like them are perhaps most useful in sequences in which some interval of a chord becomes another interval of the next. The inversions of the diminished seventh chord are to be used as in preceding lessons, in **both** major and minor.

EXERCISES TO LESSON XLI.

LESSON XLII.

CHROMATIC PASSING TONES.

When the progression of any voice by one whole step is subdivided into two half steps by the chromatic expansion or contraction of the interval, tones are introduced which are foreign to the key. Such tones may produce changes of **mode,** or even transient changes of **key ;** but in most cases, being regarded as melodic rather than harmonic, they do not affect the original relation of the chords to one another, or to the key in which they are written. Thus the chord of the diminished seventh, as used in the major mode, is the chromatic contraction of a minor into a diminished seventh. The augmented triad also belongs in the same category, being the expansion of a major triad by means of an accidental. For this reason the augmented triad was not included in the lesson on the secondary triads of the minor scale. In fact, its use in any form, excepting that of a chromatic alteration, is comparatively rare. In this form it is altered from any major triad, in both major and minor keys.

By the use of chromatic alterations, major triads become augmented or minor, minor triads become major or diminished, and seventh chords may have any of their intervals contracted or expanded without altering their original relation to the key. These alterations may also take place in more than one voice at the same time, thus forming chords identical with the fundamental harmonies of another key, and still retain their relationship to the original tonality. Thus:

178.

The chord at *a* is of course the first inversion of the supertonic seventh of G major. At *b* the third is chromatically raised, forming a chord equivalent to the dominant seventh of the key of D. At *c* the root is also raised, forming the equivalent of the diminished seventh in the key of B minor, yet the identity of the chord remains the same as before the chromatic alterations took place. This principle remains the same in the analysis of **all** chords formed by chromatic alteration.

All augmented and diminished intervals are discords requiring a resolution, the general principle of which is as follows:

The augmented tones of an interval ascend one diatonic semitone.

The diminished tones of an interval descend one diatonic semitone.

179.

Intervals chromatically altered may not be doubled, as the resolution of both voices at once would involve consecutive octaves.

Chromatic alterations are often written enharmonically, partly on account of greater simplicity of notation, and partly in order to conform to the notation of the chromatic scale, in which the seventh degree remains lowered and the fourth degree remains raised both in ascending and descending, the other degrees being raised in ascending and lowered in descending. Thus:

180.

It may be also observed that, in the harmonies formed by chromatic alteration, there are many instances of incorrect notation in the works of the greatest masters.

The following example illustrates the chromatic alteration of chords without change of key. If the chromatic passing tones are omitted, the progression from chord to chord remains the same.

1, 2, 4, 5. Fifth raised.

3. Chromatic scale written enharmonically.

6, 10. Seventh lowered.

7. Third raised.

8, 11, 12. Third lowered.

9. Fifth lowered.

13. Root raised.

EXERCISES TO LESSON XLII.

1. Figured bass given.

2.

3. Melody given.

LESSON XLIII.

MIXED CHORDS.

THE CHORDS OF THE AUGMENTED SIXTH.

The principle of chromatic alteration applied to certain intervals results in the combination of tones not found in any one key. (Such intervals as diminished and augmented thirds and sixths, doubly augmented and diminished fourths and fifths are thus formed.) Such combinations are called **mixed** or **altered** chords, and to this class belong the useful and interesting harmonies known as the **augmented sixth chords** (in some text-books styled French, German, and Italian sixths). Their distinguishing feature is the melodic contraction of the minor third into a diminished third, which being inverted becomes an augmented sixth. This is effected either by raising the lower tone or by lowering the upper tone of the original third.

When formed from a **major** third the alteration takes place **in both parts at once.**

It is from this interval of an augmented sixth that these chords derive their name. Although in the conventional usage of these chords the lower tone of the augmented sixth lies in the bass, their use in the fundamental position, and in the inversions which bring the augmented sixth between the inner voices, is by no means rare. In fact, the works of modern masters contain numberless examples of all these combinations. It may be remarked, however, that the fundamental positions and inversions involving the diminished **third** are more frequent in the form of tenths, by which their harshness is somewhat neutralized.

These chords are formed, according to the principle of chromatic alteration explained in the preceding lesson, from **any** chords which contain a minor third or major sixth, provided that the alteration of the interval consists of a whole step **divided into two half steps.** (See Lesson XLII.) Certain chords, however, are more frequently used than others for this purpose, and they may be classified as follows: The minor triad with the root raised,

182.

The minor triad and minor seventh with the root raised,

Diminished triad with the third lowered,

Diminished seventh chord with the third lowered,

Diminished triad and minor seventh with the third raised,

Dominant seventh chord with the fifth lowered,

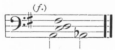

Dominant seventh chord with the fifth raised,

These chords are here given in their most familiar form (that of the augmented sixth between the bass tone and the other voices), and although they are formed in various keys in order to show their derivation, it will be seen that their augmented interval in this instance always lies between A♭ in the bass and F♯ in the soprano. The tendency of the interval of the augmented sixth is to resolve to a perfect octave, both parts moving a semitone. In fact, when the interval is formed by the alteration of **both** its tones, both tones must of course resolve. If we omit all the accidentals we shall find that these chords (excepting the last one) are formed from the chords of the IV, IV₇, and II₇, in C major, to which key they may all resolve; and inasmuch as any or all of the intervals may be altered, either singly or in combination, it follows that the relation of the chord to a given key must depend upon the alteration.

This is clearly shown at *e, f*, the first chord of which is formed by raising the third of the chord of the II₇ in C minor; the second by lowering the fifth of the chord of the V₇ in G major.

These chords will be here indicated by the Roman numerals, as in the preceding lessons, with the signs + and o added to the figures for augmented and diminished intervals.

THE AUGMENTED SIXTH CHORD.

The first inversion of triads with a diminished third, which invert into augmented sixths, is formed in two ways, as seen in Example 182, *a* and *c*.

First, by raising the root of a minor triad in a major key

from either the chord of the supertonic or the submediant, but not of the mediant, because the raised root of the latter would resolve **out of the key.** In minor it may be formed either from the chord of the subdominant or the tonic.

Second, by lowering the third of a diminished triad

185.

from either the chord of the leading tone of a major or minor key, or from that of the supertonic in minor. The latter form, however, is not usual.

The fifth of the chord is doubled, either in unison or octaves, and one of the fifths must be below the root. For this reason the chord of the augmented sixth cannot well be used in the fundamental position. In harmonizing melodies the position formed by lowering the second degree of the scale is often used, instead of the dominant $\frac{6}{4}$ $\frac{}{3}$ chord. (See exercises.)

It is by no means to be understood that an altered chord is necessarily preceded by its **unaltered** form, i. e. by the chord from which it is derived. An altered chord may be preceded by any chord from which a legitimate progression can be made, its relationship to a key being established by its resolution.

186.

EXERCISES TO LESSON XLIII.

The sign + indicates where the augmented chord is to be introduced.

These cadences are to be played in every key.

LESSON XLIV.

MIXED CHORDS. (Continued.)

THE AUGMENTED SIX-FIVE CHORD.

If to the minor triad with raised root, or to the diminished triad on the leading tone in minor with lowered third, explained in Lesson XLIII, we now add another third, there results the altered seventh chord, whose first inversion is known as the chord of the augmented sixth and fifth.   The **first-mentioned** form is found, of course, on the intervals of the supertonic, mediant, and submediant in major, and on the subdominant in minor.   Of these chords the mediant is not available, from the fact that the augmented root resolves out of the key. (See Lesson XLIII .)

The chords on the subdominant in minor (see Example 187, *a*) and of the supertonic in major (see Example 187, *b*) are the most useful, on account of their direct resolution, with a stationary seventh, to the tonic triad.

The **second-mentioned** form is simply a chord of the diminished seventh with the third lowered,

It will be remembered that the third of the vii°₇ is not allowed to descend when below the seventh, on account of the consecutive fifths involved. If, then, this third be lowered, it must descend; therefore, this chord cannot be used in the first inversion ($\frac{6+}{5}$), as the third would descend in parallel fifths with the seventh (Example 187, *c*). It may be noted, however, that these parallel fifths are often to be found in masterworks, especially in those of Mozart. They are still more often avoided when the third is below the seventh, by first resolving the seventh a semitone downward,

188.

then the rest of the chord.

These same consecutive fifths are also formed when the augmented $\frac{6}{5}$ chord, derived from the iv₇ in minor, resolves to the dominant triad,

189.

and these are likewise avoided by first resolving the seventh.

190.

This forms temporarily another form of augmented sixth chord (the chord of the augmented six-four-three or $\frac{6+}{4}$), which will be considered later. The following summary shows the augmented six-five chord, with its possible derivations and resolutions in major and minor. The form at 4 is less usual than the others.

SUMMARY.

The fundamental positions, as well as the second and third inversions, of this chord are entirely practicable and are analyzed in Lesson XLVIII.

EXERCISE TO LESSON XLIV.

Exercise including modulation.

The augmented $\frac{6}{5}$ chord is indicated by a + in the following exercises.

Play in every major key.

LESSON XLV.

MIXED CHORDS. (Continued.)

THE CHORD OF THE DOUBLY AUGMENTED FOURTH.

The enharmonic equivalent (or one of them) of the augmented $\frac{6}{5}$ chord is formed by adding a major third, doubly augmented fourth, and augmented sixth to a given bass tone.

191.

Thus the interval A♭–D♯ corresponds enharmonically to the perfect fifth A♭–E♭ of the augmented sixth chord explained in the previous lesson.   This chord is formed:

First, by lowering the fifth of a diminished seventh chord (see Example 192, *a*) ;

Second, by lowering the fifth of a minor triad with minor seventh, and raising the root and third **at the same time.** (Example 192, *b*.) In this form (the most useful one) it resolves to the $\frac{6}{4}$ tonic or dominant chord, according to its derivation.   Thus:

a.   The third inversion of the diminished seventh in *e* minor, with the fifth chromatically lowered.

b.   The third inversion of the supertonic seventh of C major, with the fifth lowered, root and third raised.

c.   The same on the submediant of F major.

The other minor seventh chords are not available for forming this chord, from the fact that the altered intervals resolve out of the key.

In the following exercises the altered chord is often *preceded*, as well as succeeded, by the $\frac{6}{4}$ tonic chord.

EXERCISES TO LESSON XLV.

MODEL.

+ Augmented triad.

Add the inner parts.

LESSON XLVI.

MIXED CHORDS. (Continued.)

THE CHORD OF THE AUGMENTED SIX-FOUR-THREE.

The augmented six-four-three chord proper is erected upon any given tone by adding a major third, augmented fourth, and augmented sixth, and is derived from the second inversion of several seventh chords, viz. :

I. From a dominant seventh chord by lowering the fifth (Example 193, *a*).

II. From a diminished triad with minor seventh by raising the third (Example 193, *b*).

III. From a minor triad with a minor seventh by lowering the fifth and raising the third at the same time (Example 193, *c*).

The first form (*a*) belongs to both the major and minor modes.

The second form (*b*) is founded on the II$_7$ in minor, resolving to the dominant triad or tonic $\frac{6}{4}$ chord, and on the VII$^0_7$o in major, resolving to the tonic or tonic $\frac{6}{3}$ chord.

The third form (*c*) is founded on either the II$_7$, III$_7$, or VI$_7$ in major, and resolves the seventh downward, while the root remains stationary.

The following model illustrates the use of this chord in its various derivations. Every accidental in this example may be omitted without affecting any of the harmonic progressions, therefore the logical conclusion is that these tones foreign to the original key are not modulating tones, and do not in any way affect the original tonality, excepting as melodic passing tones.

NOTE. The altered chord is indicated by $\frac{6+}{4+}$
3

Although this apparently contradicts the principle stated at the beginning of our lessons in modulation (see Lesson XXV), that the dominant seventh and diminished seventh chords are related to one tonality only, the fact of their being formed by **melodic alteration** causes them to lose something of their harmonic significance; otherwise we must recognize the chords at Example 194, *b*, *c*, and *d*, as the dominant sevenths of D, E, and A, with their fifths lowered, to none of which keys do they resolve.

In the exercises to be harmonized the sign + indicates where the $\frac{6+}{4}$
3 is to be introduced.

EXERCISES TO LESSON XLVI.

1. Unfigured bass.

Change the positions in the melody freely.

LESSON XLVII.

MIXED CHORDS. (Continued.)

THE NEAPOLITAN SIXTH.

When the root of the supertonic triad in minor is chromatically lowered in progressing toward the tonic, a major triad is formed, popularly known as the **Neapolitan sixth** (indicated by N^6).

195.

It is most commonly introduced as a chord of the sixth with the third doubled, resolving to the tonic $\frac{6}{4}$ or dominant chord, with or without the seventh.   Sometimes, also, the resolution is to a dominant minor ninth chord, especially if the fifth of the chord lies in the soprano voice, thus preparing the ninth.

196.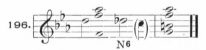

Both the fundamental position with the root doubled (see Example 197, *a*) and the second inversion with the third doubled (see Example 197, *b*) are occasionally used, and all the positions of the chord may be used in the major mode by the simultaneous lowering of the root and fifth of the supertonic triad.   (See Example 197, *c*.)

197.

NOTE. Such positions as *a*, *b*, are not really sixth chords.

Like all the altered chords previously explained, it is not in the least indispensable that the Neapolitan sixth should be preceded by its **unaltered** form. It may be preceded by any chord which progresses legitimately to the supertonic triad, giving the preference, possibly, to those of the subdominant and tonic. Numberless examples of this chord in all its forms are found in the works of the masters since the time of Bach. Though somewhat stereotyped in effect, it is expressive and often very useful in harmonizing certain chromatic progressions, as for example :

When it resolves directly to the dominant chord, the otherwise awkward interval of a diminished third —

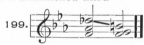

is often written, if it does not occur in the inner voices. This is illustrated at *b* in the following model :

a. First inversion, third doubled.
b. Fundamental position, root doubled.
c. Second inversion, third doubled.

EXERCISES TO LESSON XLVII.

(3 chords.)

(3 chords.)

(3 chords.)

LESSON XLVIII.

ALTERED CHORDS WITH A DIMINISHED THIRD.

The chords of the seventh containing a diminished third, from which the augmented sixth chords are derived by inversion, are freely

used in the fundamental position, as well as in the inversions not already explained. As stated in Lesson 43, the **triad** with a diminished third and fifth is not practicable in the fundamental position,
as its fifth must be below the root. (See Lesson XLIII.) In the
second inversion, however, ($\frac{6}{4}$) it is occasionally utilized *en passant*.

201.

The chord with diminished third, fifth, and seventh is the enharmonic equivalent of the dominant seventh, and is therefore of
special value as a modulating chord, as will be more fully demonstrated hereafter.

202.

a is V_7 of, and resolves to, B♭: I.
b is IV$\frac{6+}{5}$ of, and resolves to, a: I.

Since the seventh of this chord is a perfect fifth above the third,
consecutive fifths result from a resolution to the dominant. (See
Table I, *b*, 3.)

NOTE. These particular fifths are not especially bad, being in the inner voices.

Such fifths are avoided by placing the third of the chord above the
seventh (see Table I, *a*, 2, 3, 6, *b*, 4, 5, 6, etc.), in which case
it may resolve to either the tonic or dominant triad. Observe that
the interval of the diminished third or tenth invariably resolves to a
perfect unison or octave.

TABLE I.

The chord with major third, diminished fifth, and minor seventh, whose second inversion is a chord of the $\frac{6+}{4}$, resolves in all positions and inversions to a tonic or dominant chord.

The positions in which the *third lies below the fifth* are very harsh, but may be improved by transposing the third into a tenth (see Table II, *b*, all positions, also *a*, 1, 5, *c*, 3, 4, 5). All the other positions are entirely practicable and in common use by all modern composers.

TABLE II.

In the harmonizing of melodies involving the tones of the **melodic** minor scale, the raised sixth degree in ascending and lowered seventh degree in descending are to be considered as melodic alterations.

The enharmonic form of the preceding chord, formed with a minor third, **doubly** diminished fifth, and diminished seventh, is also useful in modulating, as its resolution is invariably to the tonic triad of a major key. As before, the diminished third resolves to the perfect unison. The positions and inversions are as follows:

TABLE III.

We have treated the subject of chromatic alterations and the chords derived from them thus specifically and exhaustively, because the principle involved is one of the most important with which we have to do. Innumerable other combinations may be formed in the same way, in which the dominant seventh and ninth with the fifth raised is of frequent occurrence.

The student is recommended to study out such combinations for himself.

A knowledge of the preceding tables is indispensable for the analysis of modern compositions.

EXERCISES TO LESSON XLVIII.

1. Soprano and bass given.

5. Melody alone given.

LESSON XLIX.

ENHARMONIC CHANGES.

It has been already shown (in Lesson XLV) that the dominant seventh chord coincides enharmonically with the mixed chords $\overset{6+}{4+}$ and $\overset{6+}{5}$.

Both of these altered chords, in their most natural relation ($\text{IV}\overset{+}{7}$ in minor and $\text{II}+\overset{7}{5}\text{o}$ in major) resolve to the tonic $\overset{6}{4}$ chord of the minor

or major key **one half step below** that of the corresponding dominant seventh.

For example

205.

$D\flat$: V_7 I c: IV^{6+}_{5} i C: $II^{6+}_{4++}{}_{3}$ I

If now, all the tonic triads are connected with these altered chords,
as they have already been connected with the corresponding dominant
sevenths, a new and complete series of modulations is formed. (See
Table). Thus with one chord and its enharmonic equivalent, modulations are formed to any given key and to that of a semitone below.

TABLE.

C $c\sharp$ or C $D\flat$ C d or

C D C $e\flat$ or C $E\flat$

C e or C E C f or

Transpose this table into all keys.

The diminished seventh chord, on account of its peculiar construction, is more subject to enharmonic treatment than any other chord. If the twelve semitones of the chromatic scale be divided at any point into four equal parts, the dividing tones form the intervals of a diminished seventh chord:

and since there are but three points where this can begin (without reiteration), it follows that there are but three **fundamental** diminished seventh chords *in sound*. If we include $a\sharp$ minor, each one of these has five enharmonic forms.

The other two diminished seventh chords may be analyzed in the same way.

Thus it is seen that every inversion of a diminished seventh chord is equivalent to another inversion or fundamental position of **some other** diminished seventh chord.

As all of these positions and inversions **sound** alike, the identity of the chord can only be established by finding the leading tone upon which the chord is founded (see Lesson XXII) and upon which its legitimate resolution depends.

The diminished seventh chord in all its forms is much used as an altered chord, and many irregular resolutions are thereby accounted for.

Another peculiarity is its capacity for progressing chromatically or diatonically by parallel motion in all parts at once.

By lowering any one of its intervals a chord is formed enharmonically equivalent to the V_7, $\frac{6+}{5}$, or $\frac{6+}{4}{3}$.

This of course is simply the resolution of a dominant minor ninth to the root of a dominant seventh chord.

NOTE. The entire chromatic scale harmonized in diminished seventh chords is so written that every fourth chord is in the same key, viz.:

This is in order to conform to the notation of the chromatic scale, in which the fourth degree is raised and the seventh degree lowered, both in ascending and descending.

213.

LESSON L.

IRREGULAR RESOLUTIONS OF THE DOMINANT SEVENTH CHORD.

Besides the regular resolution of the dominant seventh chord to the tonic triad there are many irregular ones, which, however, are governed by one general principle of progression. The dominant seventh may progress to any other chord:

First, with which it has tones in common; or,

Second, if the parts move only one whole or half step.

Consecutive fifths and octaves, augmented intervals and false relations are of course to be avoided, as always. The seventh may remain stationary or become enharmonically changed,

214.

or it may ascend diatonically when it is resolved in some other voice,

215.

or chromatically as an altered interval. (In this case it is often an enharmonic form of augmented sixth chord.)

It may also descend as in the regular resolution.

Thus we see that the dominant seventh chord may progress:

First, to any triad of its own key;

Second, to any seventh chord of its own key;

Third, to the tonic triad of any other key;

219.

C: V₇ I   C:V₇ D:I   A   E   B   F♯

Better.

C   D♭   A♭   E♭   B♭   F

* Really an enharmonic form of **6+**.
                                        5

Fourth, to the dominant seventh chords of any other key;

220.

C:V₇ G:V⁴₃ D:V⁴₂   A:V⁶₅   E:V⁴₂   B:V₇ ⁶₅ B:V⁶₅

F♯:V⁴₃ G♭:V⁴₃ D♭:V⁴₂ A♭:V⁶₅ B♭:V⁶₅ E♭:V⁴₂ F:V⁴₃

Fifth, and to the diminished seventh chords of any other key;

(a.) 1.   2.   3.

221.

a   b♭   b

It will be observed that these four series of dominant and diminished seventh connections are identical in sound, although the diminished seventh chords are derived from, and resolved to, every possible key.

This table should be studied at the pianoforte with every dominant seventh chord in all its complete positions, at first:

Vertically:—*a*, I; *b*, I; *c*, I; *d*, I; etc., then

Horizontally:—*a*, 1, 2, 3; *b*, 1, 2, 3; etc.; until it is thoroughly mastered in all keys. It is of great assistance in acquiring that facility in modulation so indispensable to the pianist and organist.

Many of the consecutive dominant seventh chords may be continued in the form of sequences, even those not related in tonality.

222.

The chords of the ninth and of the secondary seventh are also subject to irregular resolutions (sometimes called deceptive progressions), which may be explained on the ground of affinity of key, or of chromatic alteration.

LESSON LI.

MODULATION A MINOR SECOND UPWARD.

Returning now to the subject of modulation, we will consider the changes of unrelated or distantly related keys. Of these the modulations upward and downward a diatonic semitone (minor second) are perhaps the most important, although somewhat abrupt. Like the modulations already given, they are effected through the dominant and diminished sevenths, and also through the augmented sixth chords. (See Lesson XLIX.)

In modulating upward a minor second through the dominant seventh, the **root** of the original tonic becomes the **third** of the modulating chord; the **third** by being lowered a chromatic semitone becomes the **fifth** of the modulating chord; the **fifth** by being lowered a chromatic semitone becomes the **seventh** of the modulating chord.

The modulating chord is to be used only in the fundamental position for the present.

With the dominant seventh.

223.

In modulating upward a minor second through the diminished seventh chord the connections are as follows:

The **root** of the original tonic becomes the root of the modulating chord.

The **third** and **fifth** are chromatically lowered, and the seventh is added to the chord.

The diminished seventh of the modulating chord in this case is often written enharmonically, thereby apparently avoiding the augmented second caused by the descent from the root of the original tonic chord.

With the diminished seventh.

224.

The inversions of the diminished seventh chord are not to be used for the present.   Both of these modulations may be continued indefinitely in the form of sequences.

225.

etc.

226.

etc.

After these modulations have been thoroughly learned in all keys with the cadences, they may be reviewed in sequence form.

EXERCISES TO LESSON LI.

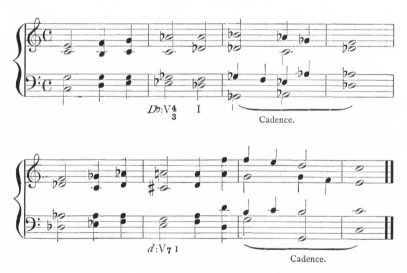

Omit no necessary accidentals.

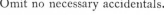

1. Unfigured bass.

Db:V$_7$

2.   5

Eb:V$_7$

3.   3

Ab:V$_7$ VI

4. Melody given.

5.

6.

7.

8.

V$_7$ V$_7$ V$_7$

LESSON LII.

MODULATION A MINOR SECOND DOWNWARD.

The modulation downward a diatonic semitone (the reverse of the preceding one), is effected through the dominant seventh, preferably in its first or second inversion, as follows:

The **third** of the original tonic becomes the **seventh** of the modulating chord.

The **fifth** descends a semitone to the **root** of the modulating chord.

One root is raised chromatically, becoming the **fifth** of the modulating chord.   The **other root** descends a diminished third, to the **third** of the modulating chord.

This awkward interval may be avoided by interposing a passing tone.   (See Ex. 227.)

227.

The second inversion of the dominant seventh chord ($\frac{4}{3}$) may be used with equal advantage.

228.

The modulation with the diminished seventh is somewhat smoother than that with the dominant seventh, on account of the two connecting tones between the tonic and the modulating chord.

The **third** and **fifth** of the original tonic become the **fifth** and **seventh** of the diminished seventh chord. **One root** is raised chromatically, becoming the **third** of that chord, while the **other root** descends a diminished third, becoming the **root** of the diminished seventh chord. The passing tone may be interposed as before.

Consecutive fifths must be guarded against in the resolution of the diminished seventh chord, when the third is below the seventh. (See Lesson XX.) The descent of the third in Example 229, *b* and *c*, may now be freely used. This modulation, like the preceding one, may be continued in the form of a sequence.

It may also be combined with the preceding, forming a modulation upward or downward a diatonic semitone, and returning to the original key.

231.

232.

Both the sequences given above, and Examples 231 and 232 are to be transposed at the pianoforte into every major key.

EXERCISES TO LESSON LII.

1. Melody given.

Sequence.

Sequence.

N^6

* The rests indicate where the melody is not to be accompanied.

LESSON LIII.

MODULATIONS OF AN AUGMENTED FOURTH OR A DIMINISHED FIFTH.

This, the most abrupt of all modulations, is easily effected through the third inversion of the dominant seventh chord, with all the upper voices progressing in contrary motion to the bass.

Even in this restricted form the fifth of the tonic triad must always be below the root, otherwise parallel fifths result, as at Example 233, *a*, *b*, *c*. The use of any inversion or fundamental position of the dominant seventh chord involves parallel fifths, augmented seconds, or still more undesirable false relations, as shown in Example 234. (See note to Lesson XXV.)

This modulation may also be made through the chord of the diminished seventh. Its harshness may be justified by the very slight movement of the three upper voices, none of which progress more than two half steps. As in the preceding lesson, the diminished seventh of the modulating chord is often written enharmonically.

Since the intervals of an augmented fourth and diminished fifth are enharmonically equivalent, it is evident that a modulation covering these intervals has only to be transposed, with the tonic triads reversed, to return to the original key. For example:

C to F$\sharp$ = augmented fourth; F$\sharp$ to B$\sharp$ = augmented fourth, B$\sharp$ = C; or, C to G$\flat$ = diminished fifth, G$\flat$ to D$\flat\flat$ = diminished fifth, D$\flat\flat$ = C.

This is shown in the following model.

236.

Since, then, the enharmonic octave is divided into two equal parts by the intervals of an augmented fourth or diminished fifth, the following series of modulations is sufficient to represent all the major keys.

1. C–F$\sharp$(G$\flat$)–C.
2. D$\flat$–G–D$\flat$.
3. D–A$\flat$–D.
4. E$\flat$–A–E$\flat$.
5. E–B$\flat$–E.
6. F–B–F.

These may be combined in turn with the modulations upward and downward a semitone, viz :

C–F$\sharp$–C–D$\flat$–G,etc. ; or,C–F$\sharp$–C–B–F,etc. ; or,C–F$\sharp$–G–D$\flat$–D, etc.

All these modulations should be carefully studied at the pianoforte.

––––––––––

LESSON LIV.

MODULATION IN GENERAL. KEY RELATION.

The modulations already given have not included changes of key between different **modes**, excepting the immediate relations of a given tonic. But since the modulating chords (the dominant and diminished seventh) may be preceded by and resolved to both major and minor tonics, the modulations already given are sufficient to cover all changes of key.   In the modulations between sharp and flat keys many **enharmonic** changes occur, the diminished seventh chord being often so changed for convenience' sake.   As keys are related in proportion to the number of tones in common between them, the difference in the number of accidentals in the signature of any two keys exactly represents their difference in tonality.

NOTE. And also their tonal distance from the natural key — the flat keys being equivalent to those with more than six sharps, and the sharp keys being equivalent to those of more than six flats.

If, then, we consider the keys of G♭ and F♯ major, and of E♭ and D♯ minor, to be identical, which is the case in the tempered scale, we form a circle of keys leading in one direction from the natural key to that of six sharps, and in the other direction from the natural key to that of six flats.

237.

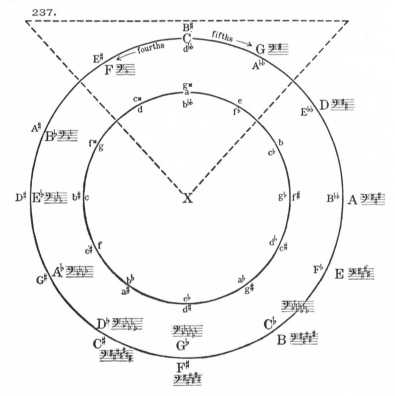

The outer circle represents the series of major keys, with their signatures; the inner one that of the minor.

NOTE. Keys which include more than seven sharps and flats cannot be indicated, since there are no signatures for them, but such keys often occur in composition, especially in modulations where enharmonic changes are undesirable.

238,

Starting from any point in the large circle, the next following key to the right is that of a fifth above: (i. e. it stands in the relation of a dominant). The next following key to the left is that of the fifth below: (i. e. subdominant). The three keys indicated by small letters on the small circle are the parallel minors of the same, and the six keys included in the dotted lines represent the key of C major with what might be styled its nearest relatives. If the triangle be revolved on the axis x, the keys included in the dotted lines will bear the same mutual relations as those given above.

This diagram shows at a glance the mutual relationship of all keys to one another. It is useful in many ways for oral work in modulation, of which the following is recommended:

239.

To C Major and Minor.

I. Modulate *from* every key to C major and minor.

Then into all other major and minor keys in the same way.

240.

From C Major and Minor.

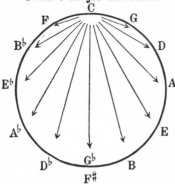

II. Modulate from C major *to* every major and minor key.

Then *from* all other major and minor keys in the same way.

III. Combine the preceding, forming a modulation from C major *to* and *from* every other major and minor key.

Then *from* all other keys in the same way.

241.

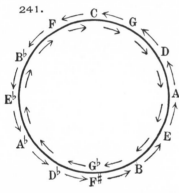

IV. Modulate by a sequence of fifths through all the major keys (C, G, D, A, etc.).

Modulate by a sequence of fourths through all major keys. (C, F, B♭, E♭, etc.).

Then through all minor keys.

242.

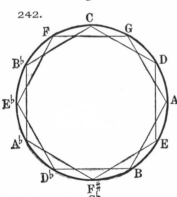

V. Modulate by sequences of major seconds in both directions, and in two series:

C, D, E, F♯, etc., C, B♭, A♭, G♭, etc., and G, A, B, etc., G, F, E♭, etc.

The same through the minor keys.

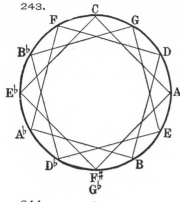

243.

VI. Modulate by sequences of minor thirds in both directions, and in three series:

C, E♭, G♭, A, C. ⎫ and in the
D♭, E, G, B♭, D♭. ⎬ reverse di-
D, F, A♭, B, D. ⎭ rection.

The same through the minor keys.

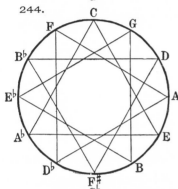

244.

VII. Modulate by sequences of major thirds in both directions, and in four series:

C, E, A♭, C.
D♭, F, A, D♭.
D, G♭, B♭, D.
E♭, G, B, E♭.

The modulation by sequences of semi-tones is given in Lessons LI and LII.

MODULATION BY TONIC CHORDS.

Although an exhaustive system of modulation by the connection of dominant and diminished seventh chords is here completed, our studies are by no means finished. Practically, **any** chords may be utilized to effect a change of key. The secondary triads (as well as their seventh chords), being neutral or ambiguous in tonality (i. e. belonging to more than one key), are identified as real tonics by the keys into which they lead. For example:

245.

C:I   d: I   II7   I⁶₄   V7   I
Not C:II   d:II7

TABLE.

This shows that tonic triads may succeed one another and form a permanent modulation, if succeeded by a complete cadence. The following table shows how this applies to all successions of major tonics, on account of their mutual relationship to the same key. (See Lesson XXV.)

EXPLANATION.

1, C major I and V; 2, G major IV and V; 3, Parallel and tonic major of *a* minor; 4, Parallel major and dominant of *a* minor; 5, *e* minor VI and V; 6, N^6 and V of *b* minor (see note); 7, V and VI of *f* minor; 8, Dominant and parallel major of *f* minor; 9, Tonic and parallel major of *c* minor; 10, F major V and IV; 11, F major V and I.

NOTE. The corresponding succession of C and F♯ at No. 6 occurs whenever the Neapolitan sixth is followed by a dominant chord. The derivation of the Neapolitan sixth in this case is as follows:

246.

b: I   I⁶   II⁰   N⁶   V

and its continuation as a permanent modulation through the minor subdominant is as follows:

247.

C:I b:N⁶   V F♯:IV   I⁶₄   V₇   I

CIRCLES OF KEYS.

The entire series of circles of keys shown in diagrams 239 to 244 should now be studied as **tonic** successions.

The circles of the fifth and fourth are shown at Example 241.

The circles of major thirds are shown at Example 244.

The circles of minor thirds are shown at Example 243.

NOTE. A key may be established by a cadence at any of the points on these circles, forming a permanent modulation.

Finally, it is not the case that all modulations must take place by the most direct means. In practical composition keys are finally changed by modulations *through other keys*, thus avoiding both abruptness and monotony. The shortest road between the two keys is not always the best from an artistic point of view; but one who knows the shortest road will surely know the longest. A general principle for modulating to a given key through other keys is as follows:

Choose connecting keys which tend in the direction of the new key to be established, by adding sharps or flats to the signature.

In this connection the following table may be found useful.

TABLE.

I to V adds one sharp to (or removes one flat from) the signature.

I to IV adds one flat to (or removes one sharp from) the signature.

I up a minor third adds three flats to (or removes three sharps from) the signature.

I down a minor third adds three sharps to (or removes three flats from) the signature.

I up a major third adds four sharps to (or removes four flats from) the signature.

I down a major third adds four flats to (or removes four sharps from) the signature.

This is illustrated by diagrams 230 to 244.

Play this table, beginning on each major tonic triad successively, and succeed the second triad with a complete cadence.

LESSON LV.

THE NON-HARMONIC TONES.

Since the tones of a chord are called **harmonic** tones, the non-harmonic tones may be defined as **tones combined with a harmony to which they do not belong.** A chord being a combination of tones derived from thirds (see Lesson I), its non-harmonic tones are those which lie between or adjacent to those of the chord. (Harmonic tones.)

The non-harmonic tones are divided into several classes, according to the relation which they bear to the harmonic tones, viz : the suspension, the anticipation, the appoggiatura, the passing tone, the embellishment, the changing tone, and the pedal or organ point.

SUSPENSIONS.

A suspension is a temporary dislocation of any interval or intervals of a chord. It is caused by delaying the diatonic downward or upward progression of any voice during a change of chords, forming a **suspended** tone foreign to the harmony.

Thus, the tone **c** (1), the root of the triad of C, is delayed in its progression to **b** (3), the third of the dominant seventh, by being **suspended** (at 2) in the tenor voice while the rest of the harmony changes, thus **dislocating** temporarily the third of the dominant seventh chord.   The three tones in question are named the **preparation** (1), the **suspension** (2), and the **resolution** (3).

Any interval may be suspended in any voice, provided that it eventually progresses diatonically.

Strictly speaking the seventh of the dominant chord cannot be suspended, for the reason that it **simply adds another third** to an existing triad.   But in combination with other suspended intervals it has the effect of a true suspension.

At *a* the progression of the soprano adds a seventh to the dominant chord, while

At *b* the seventh and fifth of the dominant seventh are practically suspended, even though the mediant triad is temporarily formed.

The preparation, in strict writing, is not allowed to be shorter (in time value) than the suspension, but as this is purely a question of rhythm, it is not necessary to observe the rule here, excepting when the preparation and suspension are tied.

The suspension occurs on the accented beat, although not necessarily on the strongest accent.   On the other hand, the resolution is always unaccented.

Since the suspension of any interval which is doubled must inevitably form a dissonant seventh or ninth, and since a ninth must never lie less than nine degrees above a root (see Lesson XIX), the following rules must be observed:

RULE 1. *The resolution of a suspension may appear simultaneously with it, if it is a ninth below the suspension, but the suspension and resolution must not appear simultaneously in the same octave.*

It is even better to avoid the doubling of suspended intervals whenever possible, by the use of other positions and inversions, and for the reason that the leading tone is seldom doubled, —

RULE 2. *The leading tone is not suspended when already present in some other voice.*

RULE 3. *The resolution of a suspension in the bass must not be doubled in an upper voice.*

The suspension may or may not be connected by a tie.

EXERCISES TO LESSON LV.

a. Fifth suspended.
b. Root suspended.
c. Third suspended.
d. Seventh doubled temporarily.

5. Suspensions in the bass.

LESSON LVI.

SUSPENSIONS. (Continued.)

Suspensions may occur in more than one voice at the same time (double and triple suspensions). Such suspensions often form combinations of intervals identical with the secondary triads and chords of the seventh, especially when they resolve into one another. (See Example.)

Thus the above example is analyzed as (a) V_2, (b) IV_2, (c) III_2, (d) II_2, with each third and root suspended, instead of (a) II_5^6 V_2, (b) I_5^6 IV_2, etc. (See Lesson XL.) Such instances are very common in sequences.

In the treatment of suspensions in the inner voices it is somewhat more difficult to avoid the combination of suspension and resolution in the same octave. For this reason the given exercises are principally in close position. Rule 1 must be strictly adhered to.

In working out the following exercises first harmonize the bass **without** suspensions in the upper voices. Then alter the diatonic downward progression into prepared suspensions with their resolutions.

EXERCISES TO LESSON LVI.

a. Root and third suspended.

5. Soprano given.

LESSON LVII.

THE INVERTED SUSPENSION. (Retardation.)

The suspension resolving upward is called **retardation** or **inverted suspension.**

It is of less frequent occurrence than the regular suspension, and is most commonly found on the third or seventh degrees of the major scale, and on the second and fifth of the minor. It may, however, be formed on any degree of the scale, provided that the tone to which it progresses is not present at the same time in some other voice and in the same octave.

254.

a.   Retardation of the third.
b.   Retardation of the root.
c.   Retardation of the fifth.

Here again many combinations are formed, identical with the secondary seventh chords, as in the case of the regular suspensions. (See Lesson LVI and XL.)

The upward and downward suspensions are very often combined, forming three parts of a legitimate chords with its regular resolution. Such cases are practically the **anticipation in the bass** of the harmony to which the suspension resolves, thus:

255.

C:I   a:VII♡₇o   I

a. Root retarded, third suspended.

b. Root, third, and fifth suspended.

Or practically, the roots of the C major and A minor triads are **anticipated** in the bass. (See Lesson LVIII.)

EXERCISES TO LESSON LVII.

a. Third suspended and retarded, fifth suspended.

b. Ninth retarded.

c. Third retarded.

d. Third retarded, fifth and third suspended.

e. Root retarded and suspended.

LESSON LVIII.

THE APPOGGIATURA AND ANTICIPATION.

A suspension which enters freely, i. e. without being prepared in the preceding chord, is called an **appoggiatura**. It is resolved downward or upward one degree, like the prepared suspension, but in the latter case commonly progresses only one half step.

256.

The appoggiatura may be approached by a skip (if not unmelodic) from any tone of the preceding chord, but *not from another non-harmonic tone.* The only exception is when it moves upward or downward by a third to another appoggiatura of the same harmonic tone.

257.

The appoggiatura may appear in any voice, but is somewhat more easily assimilated by the ear when it lies in the upper voice. It may also occur in two or more voices at the same time (double and triple appoggiatura).

258.

etc.

Such combinations may often be analyzed, however, as **altered chords.**

ANTICIPATION.

An anticipation is an unaccented tone which moves to its position in a chord in advance of the other voices. It is thus the literal reverse of the suspension, becoming a non-harmonic tone by *advancing* a progression, whereas the suspension becomes non-harmonic by *delaying* one.

259.

Like the appoggiatura the anticipation may appear in two or more voices at once. (See Example 260, *a, b.*) In fact, an entire chord may appear in advance of the beat to which it naturally belongs, forming anticipations in all the voices. (See Example 260, *c.*)

260.

The anticipation is not always repeated or tied over as a harmonic tone, but may progress to another tone of the same chord. This is called **irregular anticipation.**

261.

These are sometimes called **changing** tones, or Fux' changing tones, being a license in strict counterpoint allowed by that authority.

EXERCISES TO LESSON LVIII.

a. Appoggiatura.
b. Anticipation.

NOTE: The anticipation is commonly shorter in time value than the tone which succeeds it.

LESSON LIX.

THE DELAYED RESOLUTION OF THE SUSPENSION.

The resolution of the suspension and appoggiatura, whether down-ward or upward, is often delayed by the interpolation of other tones belonging to the chord, or forming an embellishment of the resolving tone. When the suspension comes on the first beat of the measure, the resolution may be delayed until the third or fourth beat, or even longer, by devices like the following.

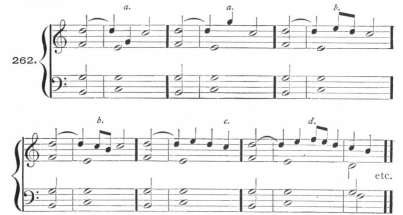

    a. Fifth of the chord interposed.

    b. Ornamental or embellished resolution.

    c. Ornamental or embellished resolution delayed until the fourth beat.

    d. Ornamental or embellished resolution delayed until the first beat of the succeeding measure.

The suspension or suspended chord is occasionally extended during a change of harmony (see Example 263, *a*, *b*),

or exchanged in position with some other voice (see Example 263,
c) ; and the harmony may be changed at the resolution of the suspension by the chromatic alteration of existing intervals, or by the
addition of sevenths to the chord, or by any other legitimate means,
which do not interfere with the original resolution of the suspension.

Here again the sequences of secondary seventh chords, (see
Lesson XXXIX) are of frequent occurrence. (See Example 264, *b.*)

EXERCISES TO LESSON LIX.

In harmonizing basses, add the suspensions after the fundamental harmony has been selected.

LESSON LX.

THE PASSING TONE AND EMBELLISHMENT.

The chromatic alterations referred to in Lesson XLII have been characterized as **melodic passing tones,** and to this class belong also the successive tones of the diatonic scale which occur between the intervals of a chord. Thus:

The **passing tone,** which, instead of proceeding to the next harmonic tone above or below, returns to the same one, is called the **embellishment.**

Many ornamental figures and melodic embellishments such as the turn, the mordent, and the trill, have their origin in such nonharmonic tones.

The **passing tone** and **embellishment** may occur in any part and between any intervals of a chord, but like the appoggiatura the **ascending** embellishment is more often by a semitone. (See Example 266.)

Consecutive perfect fifths, formed by the combination of a passing tone with a harmonic tone, are universally condemned in text-books but nevertheless written with impunity by all masters. Such fifths are often of strikingly beautiful effect. Such examples, however, should be regarded as the exceptions which prove the rule, rather than the rule itself.   Thus:

Intervals of a second between a harmonic and a passing tone should not be followed by a unison in the same voices, viz. :

and this is easily avoided by changing the direction of the voice containing the passing tones.

EXERCISES.

Harmonize the given basses with either diatonic or chromatic passing tones (half notes) in each voice in turn (three exercises to each bass), thus:

In harmonizing basses in triple rhythm two notes in each measure may be harmonic; suspensions and retardations, prepared and unprepared, may be freely introduced; the third of the chord may be temporarily omitted, and the seventh doubled on an unaccented beat.

Harmonize given basses, with three half notes in each measure, in each voice in turn (three exercises to each bass).

LESSON LXI.

ACCENTED AND DOUBLE PASSING TONES.

The accented passing tone does not differ from unprepared suspension except by being preceded by the nearest adjacent tone above **or**

below.   The following example shows the difference in effect of accented and unaccented passing tones with the same harmony.

270.

× Unaccented passing tones.
o Accented passing tones.
* Anticipation.

Accented passing tones may occur in any voice but are somewhat
less discordant when in the outer voices.   They are often combined
with other dislocations of intervals (suspensions, etc.) in same harmony.

271.   etc.

Both accented and unaccented passing tones may be written in two
voices at once.   Such double passing tones usually move in parallel
sixth and thirds or by contrary motion.

Continue the following exercises, with quarter notes in each voice,
in turn utilizing accented and unaccented passing tones and suspensions
as before.

Write each exercise three times.

1.   Continue soprano (with harmony).

etc.

* Accented passing tone in the bass combined with suspension in the alto.

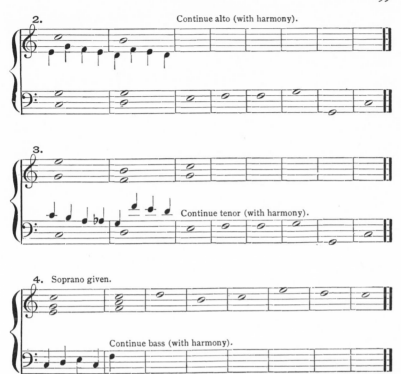

LESSON LXII.

OBLIGATO MELODY.

In the preceding lesson the notes of the running part derived from the given harmony were all of the same rhythmical value. Such a part can have but little melodic significance in the æsthetic sense, on account of its rhythmic monotony, and is, in fact, a species of counterpoint formed by embellishing the tones of the fundamental harmony.

If, however, we add to a given harmony a melody possessing rhythmic variety and interest, as well as contrapuntal accuracy, we are at once outside the proper sphere of harmony in its strictest sense.

Gounod (in his well known Ave Maria) has added a striking melody of this kind to a fundamental harmony by Bach:

272.

No arbitrary rules can be given for the construction of such melodies. The beautiful in art is not developed by rules, but by reasons, and it is hoped that the musical pupil, with the experience gained in the preceding lessons, will be able to avoid the illogical, common-place, and ugly for himself.

The cadences on pages 14, 17, 22, etc., may be used as fundamental harmonies for melodies, which for the present are to be written only in the upper voice.

Also to the following harmonies.

LESSON LXIII.

THE PEDAL OR ORGAN POINT.

A tone which is held or repeated against a series of passing chords is called a **pedal point**, or organ point.

It commonly occurs in the bass voice, but is also to be met with in the alto, tenor, or soprano. In the latter case it is sometimes called an **inverted** pedal. It is most frequently used on the **dominant** to postpone an ending:

Or on the tonic to extend and elaborate a final cadence:

In this example the pedal point is in both the upper and lower voices.

The sustained tone is used occasionally on other degrees of the scale, and sometimes on both tonic and dominant at once:

Numberless examples of such passages are to be found, especially in works of a pastoral character.

The principle involved is the same as that of combined passing tones or passing chords, the moving voices progressing independently of their connection with the sustained tone. Thus many dissonant combinations are formed, among which the dominant and diminished seventh chords on a tonic pedal (*a*) and the secondary seventh chords on a dominant pedal (*b*) are the most important.

No arbitrary limitations can be given governing the use of dissonant harmonies against the organ point. The sustained tone should be a root, third, or fifth of the first and last chords of the succession, and the intervening chords should not be so persistently dissonant as to be unsatisfactory to the ear. The more intricate the harmony, the less should the voices skip, and diatonic and chromatic scale progression are always of good effect.

The following is a stupendous example of an organ point on the dominant, from the Symphony in C minor by Brahms.

etc.

EXERCISES TO LESSON LXIII

Add the inner parts.

Add one inner part.

Harmonize, with a pedal point in any voice.

Write original periods on tonic and dominant pedals, using the exercises as models.

LESSON LXIV.

THE INVERTED PEDAL.

The organ point in the upper and inner voices is frequently used, especially in organ and choral works. The following is a beautiful example by Mendelssohn:

MENDELSSOHN.

Another one by Bach :   BACH.

279.

EXERCISES TO LESSON LXIV.

Add the inner parts.

Add *three* inner parts.

Add a pedal note and *three* other parts.

Add the tenor and bass.

4.

Add the soprano and alto.

Write original periods, with pedal notes in upper and middle voices.

LESSON LXV.

MELODIC FIGURATION.

The elaboration and embellishment of a melody by means of nonharmonic tones is called **figuration.** The nonharmonic tones are often combined with the harmonic, in arpeggio forms and otherwise, and all forms of nonharmonic tones may be utilized.

The following examples illustrate melodic variation of a given melody, the fundamental harmony remaining unchanged:

The following example shows the different species of nonharmonic tones, applied to a single given tone: (D)

All nonharmonic tones are governed by the same general law as the discords in counterpoint, viz.

I. *Accented discords must be prepared or enter from a tone of the previous chord.*

II. *Unaccented discords are introduced and resolved by diatonic succession.*

No arbitrary rules can be given for the selection of nonharmonic tones in a melodic variation. As the object is to evolve a simple and graceful melodic outline, unmelodious successions of intervals are principally to be avoided.

The given exercises are to be worked as follows:

First. Harmonize the given melody.

Second. Make a figuration of the melody, two notes to each beat, and reharmonize, retaining the original bass.

Third.   The same with four notes to each beat.

Fourth.   The same with three notes to each beat.

LESSON LXVI.

HARMONIZING OF FLORID MELODIES.

In harmonizing any embellished melody the harmonic tones must first be mentally separated from the nonharmonic ones.   The process is the exact reverse of inventing a melody for a given harmony (see Lessons LXI and LXII).   On general principles, the harmony will consist principally of the three principal triads and their inversions, with modulations to the adjacent keys.   Tones progressing by a skip are usually (though not invariably) *harmonic* in character ; the embellishment, on the other hand, being diatonic.

A melody may be simplified by omitting the ornamentation, rendering the fundamental harmony somewhat more obvious.   Thus :

In harmonizing the given exercise :

I.   Reduce the melody to its simplest form, as above.

II.   Harmonize the same, as *simply* as possible.

III.   Write the original melody with the same harmony with whatever alterations are necessitated by the part writing.

IV.   Harmonize the melody, off-hand, without reference to the studies, I, II, and III, already made.

LESSON LXVII.

ACCOMPANIMENTS.

Accompaniments are formed by representing the tones of a fundamental harmony in succession or by repetition, or as combinations of both, forming figures which are reiterated at each accented beat, or oftener. These conventional figures, of which there are practically an infinite number, trace their rhythmic origin to the broken chords and arpeggio forms in one, two, three, or even more voices. In the more idealized forms, the nonharmonic tones and embellishments are also freely combined with the tones of the chord; two (or more) figures of accompaniment may be used simultaneously; contrapuntal parts are even introduced, or secondary melodies in the form of an obligato added to the accompaniment.

The function of the accompaniment is to furnish a harmonic and rhythmic background, which shall enhance the beauty and effect of the melody itself.

Some of the more common figures of accompaniment are **as** follows. Beginning with the broken chord form, in one voice:

In two voices.

In three voices.

· With embellishment.

Two simultaneous figures.

By repetition.

The following examples are from the "Songs without Words" by Mendelssohn, which present a remarkable variety of accompaniment for lyric melodies.

1.

Form the following chords (at the pianoforte)into figures of accompaniment like the examples at 285–290.

Rewrite the following harmony in the form of an accompaniment, according to above models.

The cadences on pages 14, 17, 22, 28, and 36 may be used in the same way.

The melodies given in Lesson LXVI may now be accompanied, without altering the harmony previously written. Accompanying figures should be chosen, best adapted to the character of the melody, and each piece when completed must be possible to play.

The simpler melodies in the preceding lessons may also be used.

LESSON LXVIII.

THE CHROMATIC SCALE, HARMONIZED.

The nature of chromatic progression is such that the greatest possible scope can be given to any harmony which accompanies the chromatic scale. The simplest method is to consider each sharped or flatted tone as a chromatic alteration of one of the degrees of the diatonic scale. Thus:

Or we may modulate in sequences between the tones of the chromatic scale, regarding them as the roots of a series of tonic chords in a circle of major seconds, major and minor thirds, perfect and augmented fourths, etc. For example:

(For convenience sake the chromatic scale is here based on F.)

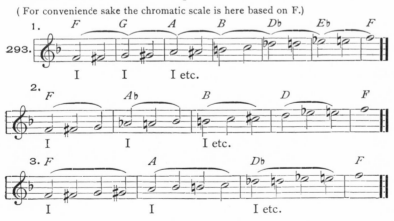

The harmony which connects the tonic chords must progress as smoothly as possible.   Each tonic chord will be immediately preceded by a dominant, or diminished seventh, or other chord of which it is the resolution, and any chord may be written enharmonically.

Continue each sequence as here indicated.   Each exercise should be carefully written out and transposed, at the Pianoforte.   The diagrams in Lesson LIV will be found useful in this connection.

Also beginning on E.

Also beginning on E and E♭.

Also beginning on G♭, G, and A♭.

4.

etc.

Continue the circle of fourths until complete.

5.

Continue in open position.

Also beginning on G♭, G, A♭, A, and B♭.

The harmony of the descending chromatic scale may be founded on the following sequences.

1.

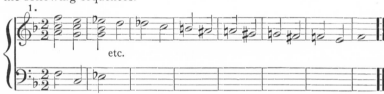

etc.

Also beginning on E.

2.

etc.

Also beginning on E and E♭.

3

etc.

Also beginning on E, E♭, and D.

Continue the circle of fourths until complete.

Also beginning on E, E♭, D, D♭, and C.

Sequences may also be formed of tonic chords in the third and fifth positions, connected by modulating chords. The student is recommended to invent such forms for himself and carry them through all the keys.

LESSON LXIX.

THE FIGURED CHORALE.

Passing tones may occur in two or more voices at once, provided that objectionable progressions (parallel fifths, octaves, etc.) are avoided.

Thus it happens that parallel thirds and sixths are of very frequent occurrence as passing voices and are sometimes combined with a fourth, forming passing chords of the sixth, and sixth and fourth. (See Lesson LXII.)

By combining the different species of nonharmonic tones, in harmonizing a given melody, the voice parts are made interesting and melodious. In fact, the licenses of progression which are allowed in part writing are entirely due to the independence and individual interest of the separate parts. Thus Bach illuminates the following simple harmony:

The following chorals are to be first worked by altering the given parts (except the soprano) with nonharmonic tones, so that a continuous rhythm of four quarter notes is present in every measure.

After which they are to be **rewritten,** with original harmony from given soprano only, continuing the motion of quarter notes in any or all voices as before.

Work out each chorale also in triple rhythm, i. e. with a continuous movement of three quarter notes in each measure. Thus:

This work may be continued indefinitely with more elaborate rhythms of quarter, eighth, and even sixteenth notes in each measure. Magnificent examples of such figured chorales are found in the organ works of J. S. Bach.

LESSON LXX.

THE FIGURED CHORALE, CONTINUED.

BASS GIVEN.

The figured chorale with given bass, presents a slight peculiarity in harmonizing, viz.: in order to form a cadence at the end of each verse line the last bass tone must invariably be the root of a triad. This leads to somewhat freer modulation than is the case when the soprano is given.

The chorales are to be worked out in the same manner as in the preceding lesson, viz.:

I.   Harmonized (as simply as possible).

II.   The same with passing tones, suspensions, embellishments, etc., in the upper voices.

III.   The same in triple rhythm with non-harmonic tones in the upper voices.

The complete chorales to be thus varied are, viz.:

LESSON LXXI.

The chorale with alto or tenor given, is to be worked in the same manner as the two preceding lessons, viz. :

I.   With simple harmony :

Chorale in alto.

II.   With nonharmonic tones in the other voices :

III.   And in triple rhythm :

The complete chorale is as follows :

No. 1.   Alto.

No. 2.

The following is to be worked the same way, in the tenor.

LESSON LXXII.

ANALYSIS.

In analyzing the given excerpts the following method is to be observed:

I.   Copy out the piece carefully.

II.   Analyze the piece harmonically, indicating the derivation of each chord and all the modulations. Chromatic changes may or may not produce modulations. In all cases define the harmony as simply as possible.

III.   Indicate carefully all the nonharmonic tones (suspensions, anticipations, organ points, etc.) and account for every tone.

The following model shows the method of writing out the analysis. This work may profitably be extended indefinitely. A comprehensive study of the chorales by Bach is earnestly recommended.

1.

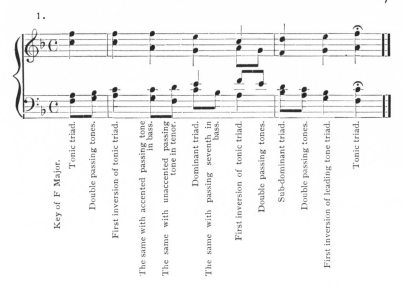

The chorale is continued as follows:

2.

Andante cantabile.

tr.

3.   *Adagio.*

WAGNER.

CONCLUSION.

The harmonic combinations formed by extending the series of thirds upwards from a given chord of the ninth, or secondary seventh (chords of ninth, eleventh, and thirteenth), have not been specially discussed in this book, for the reason that thorough practice in the use of the secondary seventh chords and suspensions has a tendency to develop these combinations in their most practicable form.

Only by experience does the student finally learn to make a virtue of necessity. Therefore, the author has not thought it necessary to reiterate warnings against hidden fifths and octaves, and against false relations, after their initial definition, preferring to leave these matters to the discretion of the intelligent teacher.

All the given lessons in the use of the nonharmonic tones may be continued indefinitely, to the great advantage of the student, especially the lessons on the figured chorale, which form in themselves the most natural introduction to the study of counterpoint or part writing.

The general laws of part writing may be briefly summarized as follows:

I. No progression is *right* if it can be altered for the better.

II. No progression is *wrong* if it cannot be altered for the better.

III. Any progression of not more than one degree which does not involve consecutive fifths, consecutive octaves, augmented seconds, or false relations, is not wrong.

IV. Between a strong progression and a strong chord, choose the strong progression.

A KEY

to

CHADWICK'S HARMONY

by the Author

G. W. CHADWICK, A.M.

DIRECTOR OF THE NEW ENGLAND CONSERVATORY OF MUSIC

BOSTON, MASS.

———

BOSTON,

THE B. F. WOOD MUSIC CO.

PREFACE.

The solutions here given are not to be regarded as the only possible harmonizations of the given basses and melodies. The student should be allowed some liberty in his choice of positions- even in his choice of the chords themselves- in proportion to his natural talent and innate musical taste. For this reason the lessons, which partake of the character of original work (LXV),have not been fully worked out.

It may be suggested that the lessons on the Figured Chorale belong to the domain of Counterpoint (in the modern sense). While this is certainly true, as far as the part-writing is concerned, such an art can never be mastered by the study of Counterpoint alone. The lessons on the Figured Chorale (especially with the melody in the inner voices) may be continued indefinitely with ever increasing profit to the student, and it is for this purpose that the 17 Chorales by Bach are given at the end of the book.

In the exercises on Analysis the harmony has been defined as simply as possible, but in many cases it is capable of other constructions, perhaps equally logical and correct.

G.W. CHADWICK.

CONTENTS.

CONTENTS.

CONTENTS.

A KEY
to
Chadwick's Harmony.

EXERCISES TO LESSON I, PAGE 6.
The Principal Triads of the Major Scale.

Note: In all exercises in which the bass, figured or unfigured, is given, much liberty may be allowed the student in the choice of position of the chords, especially in the final cadences. The solution which gives the most musical soprano must be regarded as the most desirable. The conservative teacher may find a rather free use of hidden octaves and fifths in connection with changes of positions in these exercises, but the author has chosen to be guided by the musical ear rather than the pedantic eye.

1. Soprano given.

* These exercises admit of other and equally correct solutions.

EXERCISES TO LESSON II, PAGE 9.

The Principal Triads of the Major Scale.

(Continued.)

1. Bass given.

6.

E: I — V— IV— V I— IV— V — I

EXERCISES TO LESSON III, PAGE 10.
The Principal Triads of the Minor Scale.

1. Bass given.

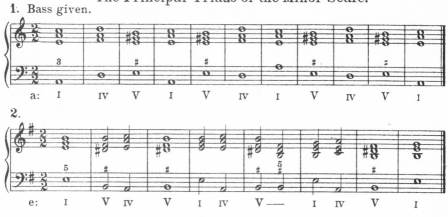

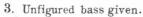

a: I IV V I V IV I V IV V I

2.

e: I V IV V I IV V — I IV V I

3. Unfigured bass given.

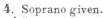

f: I V I V — IV I IV V I IV I V IV V — I

4. Soprano given.

e: I ——— V IV I V I — IV V I

5.

c: I V IV I V I IV— I IV I IV V IV I —— V I

EXERCISES TO LESSON IV, PAGE 14.
The Chord of the Sixth.

1. Bass given.

C: I -   V I   IV I   V I   IV —   V I   IV V   I

2.

e: I IV I   V———   I IV I   V   I IV—   I IV I IV V   I

3. Soprano given.

D: I   V I   I —   V   — I   IV—   I IV V   I

4.

c: I V I———   IV———   I   V I V IV—   V———   I

5.

B♭:   I—   V I   IV I   V —   I——   V I   IV I V   I

Chord of the Sixth and Fourth.

EXERCISES TO LESSON VI, PAGE 21.

The Chord of the Dominant Seventh.

1. Figured bass given.

2.

3. Unfigured bass given.

4. Soprano given.

5.

6.

First Inversion of the Chord of the Dominant Seventh.

The Second Inversion of the Chord of the Dominant Seventh.

1. Figured bass given.

D: I   V₇   I   V   I   —   IV   V₇   I   IV   I   V₇   I

2.

d: I   V₇   I   V₇   I   V₇   I   V   I —   V₇   I   V₇   I

3. Unfigured bass given.

a: I — V₇ I IV— I V I IV V–₇ I V₇ I IV—I V₇ I V₇ I

4. Soprano given.   a)

C: I V₇ V I   V I V₇ V₇ I — — IV I V₇ I V I IV V₇ I   I IV V I

+)This chord is merely interposed between the V⁴₃ and its resolution, or the measure may be harmonized as at *a*).

5.

G: I V₇ I V₇ IV I IV I V I V₇ IV₇ I — V — I V₇ I—V V₇ I—I V₇ I

6.

g: I V₇ I V₇ I — V₇ I   V₇ I—V   I V I V₇ I   IV I IV   I—V₇ I

+)See note on page 26 of **Harmony** Course.

The Third Inversion of the Chord of the Dominant Seventh.

The Secondary Triads in Major.
(The Supertonic Triad.)

1. Figured bass given.

G: I II V I IV I V₇ I V₇ I IV I V₇ I

2.

D: I V₇— I V₇ I V II IV——— V₇— I

3. Unfigured bass given.

B♭: I— V₇— I II I IV II IV V₇ I II I V₇ I

4. Soprano given.   or

A: I— II I II IV V₇ I V₇ I V₇ I II IV V₇ I V₇ I ·V₇ I V₇ I

5.

D♭: I II IV V₇ I V₇ I V V₇ I II V— I IV I V₇ I

6.

B♭: I——— II— V— I— V I V I——— IV II V I II I V₇ I

EXERCISES TO LESSON XI, PAGE 39.
The Submediant Triad.

1. Figured bass given.

+ See Example 79, page 36 in Harmony Course.

2.

3. Unfigured bass given.

4. Soprano given.

5.

6.

A: I   VI   IV V₇   VI II I V   VI IV   I——   IV II V₇ I

EXERCISES TO LESSON XII, PAGE 43.
The Mediant Triad.

1. Figured bass given.

C: I III   IV I   V—7   I——   V —   VI I   IV V₇   I

2.

A: I   V.—7 VI   III IV   I————   III IV—   V I V₇   I

3. Unfigured bass given.

Bb: I V₇ I V—7 VI IV I V   I III IV   I——   IV II V₇ I

4. Soprano given.

A: I V₇ I V—7 VI IV I V   I III IV I——   IV II V₇ I

5.

Eb: I — III IV V₇ I— IV V—7 I VI IV V I—V VI IV II V₇ I

EXERCISES TO LESSON XIII, PAGE 47.

Inversions of the Secondary Triads.

1. Figured bass.

2.

3. Unfigured bass.

4. Soprano given.

5.

+) Third doubled to avoid consecutive fifths with the next chord.

EXERCISES TO LESSON XIV, PAGE 49.

The Leading-Tone Triad.

1. Figured bass.

C: I   II   VII°   I   VI   VII°   V   I —   IV   II   I   V   I

2.

G: I   IV   VII°   III   VI   II   V7   I   — IV   II   I   V7   I

3. Unfigured bass.

D♭: I —   VII°   I   V —   VI   V   I   IV   I   VII°   I   II   V   I

4. Melody given.

A♭:   I VII° I   IV   I —   V7 I VII° I   V —   I–VII° I   IV–VII° I   V7 VI II V7   I

5.

E♭: I   IV   VII°   I—   V — 7   I—   VII°   I   V7   VI   II   V   I

Secondary Triads in Minor, with their Inversions.

1. Figured bass given.

c: I   II° I VII   I IV—   I V₇   VI——   V—I   VII°I IV   I V₇   I

2.

e: I——   IV ——   I V₇VI VII° I V₇VI   IV   IV—I — IV I V₇   I

3. Unfigured bass.

c: I V₇ VI IV   I——   VII° I   (V) V₇——   I IV   I V₇   I

4. Melody given.

d: I ——   V   V₇ I V₇——   I—— IV—   V—I   IV I V₇   I

5.

a: I VII° I II° V-₇IV₁Y₇ I—V₇I   V - I V₇VII° VI V I II° I—II°V₇ I—

Note: The musical student **may** now be encouraged to compose little melodies similar to the fore-going, harmonizing them strictly in accordance with the given **rules** and using only the material thus far required.

EXERCISES TO LESSON XVII, PAGE 65.
Dispersed Harmony (Open Position.)

1. Figured bass given.

2.

3. Unfigured bass.

4. Melody given.

5.

Compare with N⁰ 2.

EXERCISES TO LESSON XVIII, PAGE 67.

Dispersed Harmony (Open Position) in Minor.

1. Figured bass given.

2.

3. Unfigured bass.

4. Melody given.

5.

EXERCISES TO LESSON XIX, PAGE 70.

The Dominant Ninth in Major, and its Inversions.

EXERCISES TO LESSON XX, PAGE 73.

The Dominant Ninth in Minor.

The Chord of the Seventh on the Leading-Tone.

The Chord of the Diminished Seventh.

1. Melody given.

The Inversions of the Diminished Seventh Chord.

1. Figured bass given.

2.

3. Unfigured bass.

4. Given melody.

5.

✤ The fifth ascends—See 146 B, page 79.

EXERCISES TO LESSON XXIV, PAGE 82.

The Chord of the Diminished Seventh *(Continued.)*

1. Figured bass given.

24

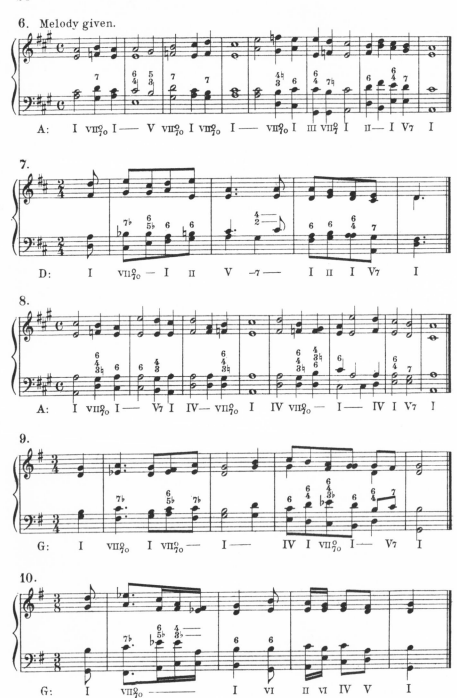

EXERCISES TO LESSON XXV, PAGE 88.

The Modulation to the Dominant.

1. Melody given.

C: I   V   I   G: V₇   I   IV   I   V₇   I

EXERCISES TO LESSON XXVI, PAGE 92.

The Modulation to the Subdominant.

Soprano given.

1. *Modulating tone in Soprano.*

2.

3. *Modulating tone in Alto.*

4. *Modulating tone in Tenor.*

5. *Modulating tone in Bass.*

Modulation between the Tonic, Dominant
and Subdominant Chords.

EXERCISES TO LESSON XXVIII, PAGE 97.
Modulation from a Major Key to its Parallel Minor.

EXERCISES TO LESSON XXIX, PAGE 100.
Modulation from a Minor Key to its Parallel Major.

EXERCISES TO LESSON XXX, PAGE 101.

Practical Modulations resulting from the preceding Lessons.

1. Soprano given.

EXERCISES TO LESSON XXXI, PAGE 105.
Modulation from a Major Key to the Parallel Minor
of its Dominant:

1. Soprano given.

C: I — V₇ I — e: V₇ I —— IV II° I V₇ I

2.

A: I IV I V—₇ VI IV II I V I—c♯: V₇ I — IV II° I V₇ I

3.

G: I—V₇ V—₇ I — V₇ I—V I —b: V₇ I V₇ I IV I IV I V₇ I

4.

F: I VII°₇₀ I —— IV I V I— a: V₇ I — IV V₇ I

5.

E♭: I IV I IV II I V ——₇ I g: VII°₇₀ I V₇ I

EXERCISES TO LESSON XXXII, PAGE 108.
Modulation from a Minor Key to the Subdominant
of its Parallel Major.

CHANT.

1. Soprano given.

c: I   IV——   V   I   A♭:VII°₇₀ I   II   I   V——7   I

2. d: I   VII°₇₀   IV VII°₇₀   I——   B♭:V₇   I   IV——   I

3. e: I ——   VII°₇₀   I   —C:V₇   I ——   V₇   I

4. f: I—— VII°₇₀ I—— V—7 V   I D♭:VII°₇₀ I IV I V₇   I

5. b: I   VII°₇₀—IV V₇——   I IV— I G:V₇ I V I IV I IV   I V₇ I

Modulation from a Minor Key to the Subdominant of its Parallel Major. *(Continued.)*

EXERCISES TO LESSON XXXIV, PAGE 112.

Modulation from a Major Key to the Parallel Minor of its Subdominant.

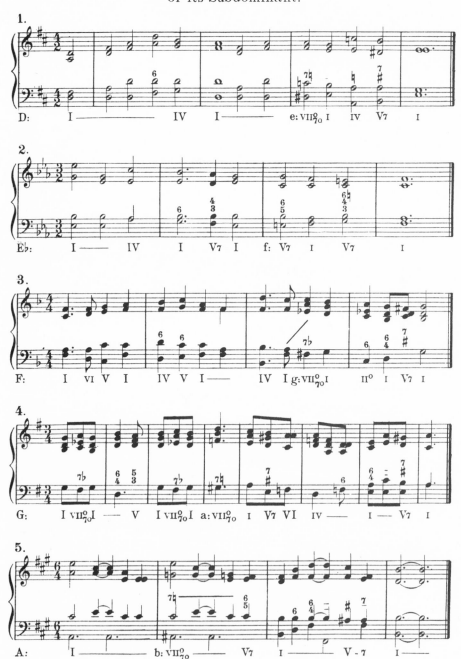

EXERCISES TO LESSON XXXV, PAGE 115.

Modulation from a Minor Key to the Dominant of its Parallel Major.

1. Soprano given.

e: I———— D: V7 — I — IV I - V7 — I

This exercise may precede or succeed N⁰ 1, page 34.

2.

f: I Eb: V7 — I V7 I IV II V7 I

This exercise may precede or succeed N⁰ 2, page 34.

3.

g: I - F: VII⁰7o I IV - V9 I VI IV I - II V7 I

4.

a: I VII⁰7o I - V I VII⁰7o I G: VII⁰7o V7 I V -7 VI II I - V7 I

5.

b: I —————— A: VII⁰7o ———— V7 I V -7 I—

This exercise may precede or succeed N⁰ 5, page 34.

36

EXERCISES TO LESSON XXXVI, PAGE 117.

Combination of the preceding Modulations.

EXERCISES TO LESSON XXXVII, PAGE 121.
The Supertonic Seventh Chord, in Major and Minor.

6. Choral. Involving Modulation.

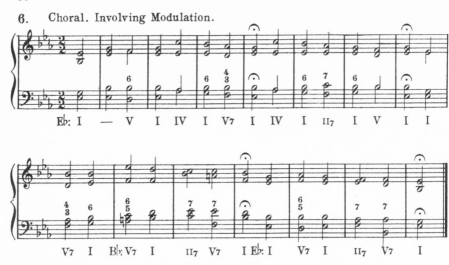

Eb: I — V I IV I V7 I IV I II7 I V I I

V7 I Bb: V7 I II7 V7 I Eb: I V7 I II7 V7 I

EXERCISES TO LESSON XXXVIII, PAGE 122.
Inversions of the Supertonic Seventh Chord.

1. Soprano given.

C: I II–7 V7 I IV I II7 V7 I ——— II7 I II7 V7 I II7 V7— I

2. Involving Modulation.

F: I — II–7 V7 — III V7 I d: V7 I Bb: V7 I F: I II7——I V7 I

3.

Ab: I V — I — II–7 I V7 I VI II–7 V7 I II7 – III V7 I

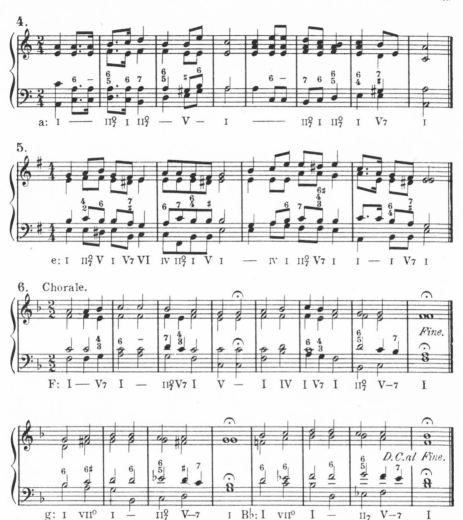

EXERCISES TO LESSON XXXIX, PAGE 125.
Secondary Seventh Chords of the Tonic, Mediant, Subdominant, and Submediant, in Major.

1. Soprano given.

EXERCISES TO LESSON XL, PAGE 127.
Secondary Seventh Chords, in Minor.

6. Chorale.

Eb: I IV I V₇ I II₇ V I c:V I VI−₇ II⁰₇ V I Eb:VI III I IV V₇ I IV

I— IV I II c:IV₇ V Eb:VI V—₇ I Bb:I II₇ V I Eb:I V₇ I II₇ V I
Bb: I−₇b IV

EXERCISES TO LESSON XLI, PAGE 129.

Inversions of the Secondary Seventh Chords,
in Major and Minor.

1. Figured bass given.

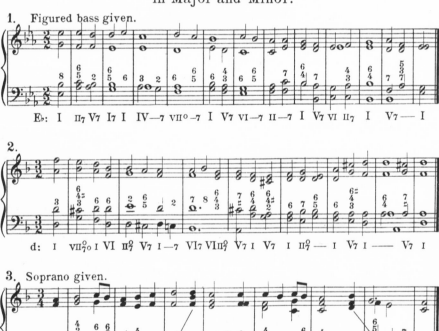

Eb: I II₇ V₇ I₇ I IV—₇ VII⁰−₇ I V₇ VI—₇ II—₇ I V₇ VI II₇ I V₇— I

2.

d: I VII⁰₇₀ I VI II⁰₇ V₇ I−₇ VI₇ VII II⁰₇ V₇ I V₇ I II⁰₇— I V₇ I —— V₇ I

3. Soprano given.

F: I II₇ V−₇ I V₇ I IV II₇ V−₇ I VI₇ II₇ V−₇ I₇ VI II₇ —— V−₇ I

EXERCISES TO LESSON XLII, PAGE 132.
Chromatic Passing Tones.

1. Figured bass given.

+ Enharmonic form for C♯

EXERCISES TO LESSON XLIII, PAGE **137.**
MIXED CHORDS.
The Chords of the Augmented Sixth.

EXERCISES TO LESSON XLIV, PAGE 141.
MIXED CHORDS.(Continued.)
The Augmented Six-Five Chord.

1. Soprano given.

EXERCISES TO LESSON XLV, PAGE 143.

The Chord of the Doubly Augmented Fourth.

1. Soprano given.

2.

3.

4. With Modulation.

5. Soprano and bass given.

6. Soprano given.

EXERCISES TO LESSON XLVI, PAGE 146.

The Chord of the Augmented Six-Four-Three.

1. Unfigured bass given.

4. With modulation.

5. Melody given.

Compare with No.1 page 147.

6.

Compare with No.2 page 147.

7.

8.

Compare with No. 3 page 147.

9. With modulation.

Compare with No. 4 page 147.

EXERCISES TO LESSON XLVII, PAGE 150.
The Neapolitan Sixth.

1. Soprano given.

EXERCISES TO LESSON XLVIII, PAGE 154.

Altered Chords with a Diminished Third.

1. Soprano and bass given.

LESSON XLIX, PAGES 155 to 160.
Enharmonic Changes.

LESSON L, PAGES 160 to 164.
Irregular Resolutions of the Dominant Seventh Chord.

EXERCISES TO LESSON LI, PAGE 167.
Modulation a Minor Second Upward.

1. Unfigured bass.

2.

3.

Another version.

4. Melody given.

Compare No. 1

5.

C: I – V₇ I V I – IV V I D♭:V₇ I II III II I V₇ I
Compare N⁰ 2

6.

A: I V₇ VI II -7 VI V I I V I B♭:V₇ VI II -7 I V9-8 I
Compare N⁰ 3   7-7

7.

E: I V₇ I IV – I – V₇ I – V I V₇ I F:V₇ – I – II I V₇ I

8.

A: I — B♭:V₇ I ——— b:V₇ I ——— C: V₇ VI II7 II V₇ I

EXERCISES TO LESSON LII, PAGE 170.
Modulation a Minor Second Downward.

1.

C: I -7 B:V₇ I -7 B♭:V₇ I -7 a:V₇ I C:VI V₇ I IV V – I ———

* These progressions in the tenor are difficult of intonation for voices. The whole exercise is to be regarded as instrumental.

LESSON LIII, PAGES **171** to **173**.

Modulations of an Augmented Fourth, or a Diminished Fifth.

LESSON LIV, PAGES **173** to **180**.

Modulation in general. Key Relation.

EXERCISES TO LESSON LV, PAGE 183.

The Non-Harmonic Tones.

Suspensions.

5. Suspensions in the bass.

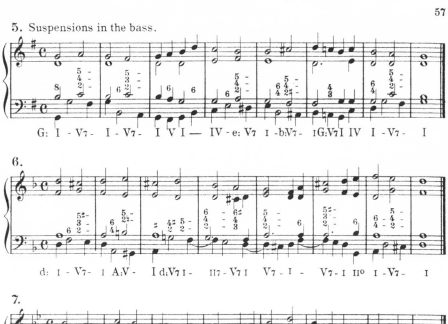

G: I - V₇ - I - V₇ - I V I — IV - e: V₇ I - b:V₇ - IG:V₇I IV I - V₇ - I

6.

d: I - V₇ - I A:V - I d:V₇I - II₇ - V₇ I V₇ - I - V₇ - I II° I - V₇ - I

7.

g: I - V - V₇ - I - V D:V₇ Ig:V₇I V I - V - I V₇ VI IV I - V₇ - I

EXERCISES TO LESSON LVI, PAGE 185.
Suspensions *(Continued.)*

1. Bass given.

D: I V₇ - VI - A:V - ₇ I D: I - ₇ IV - I - VII° I II₇ VI II I - V₇ - I

2.

c: I II₇ V - ₇ I - IV - ₇ V₇ - I V IG:VII° I c: V - ₇ I - IV - I - ₇ IV - V₇ - I

EXERCISES TO LESSON LVII, PAGE 188.
The Inverted Suspension (Retardation).

1. Melody given.

EXERCISES TO LESSON LVIII, PAGE 191.
The Appoggiatura and Anticipation.

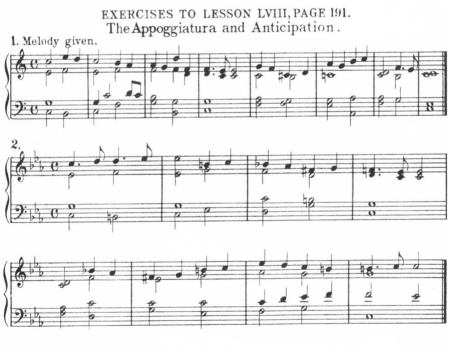

EXERCISES TO LESSON LIX, PAGE 194.

The Delayed Resolution of the Suspension.

1. Bass given.

2. Suspensions in all parts.

3.

4.

5.

6. Soprano given.

Compare № 1

7.

Compare № 2

8.

Compare No 3.

9.

Compare No 4.

10.

Compare No 5.

EXERCISES TO LESSON LX, PAGE 196.

The Passing Tone and Embellishment.

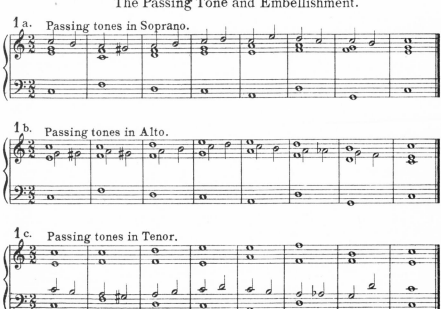

1 a. Passing tones in Soprano.

1 b. Passing tones in Alto.

1 c. Passing tones in Tenor.

2 a.   Passing tones in Soprano.

2 b.   Passing tones in Alto.

2 c.   Passing tones in Tenor.

3 a.   In triple rhythm, passing tones in Soprano.

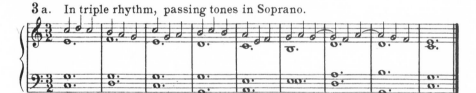

3 b.   Passing tones in Alto.

3 c.   Passing tones in Tenor.

4 a. Passing tones in Soprano.

4 b. Passing tones in Alto.

4 c. Passing tones in Tenor.

EXERCISES TO LESSON LXI, PAGE 198.
Accented and Double Passing Tones.

1. Bass given. Quarter notes in Soprano.

2. Quarter notes in Alto.

3. Quarter notes in Tenor.

4. Soprano given. Quarter notes in bass.

EXERCISES TO LESSON LXII, PAGE 200.
Obligato Melody.

1.

2.

3.

Such exercises may be continued indefinitely.

EXERCISES TO LESSON LXIII, PAGE 204.
The Pedal, or Organ Point.

1. Inner parts added.

2.

Same, with low tenor.

3.

Same, with low tenor.

4. One inner part added.

5.

EXERCISES TO LESSON LXIV, PAGE 206.
The Inverted Pedal.

1. Inner parts added.

2.

3.

Compare N⁰ 2.

4. Tenor and bass added.

5.

6.

EXERCISES TO LESSON LXV, PAGE 210.
Melodic Figuration.

1a. Melody harmonized.

1b. Figuration of Melody, harmonized with same bass.

1c. Same with four notes to each beat.

1d. Same with three notes to each beat.

2a. Melody harmonized.

2b. First Figuration.

2c. Second Figuration.

2d. Third Figuration.

Note: The above serve merely as models for the pupil in the working out of the remaining exercises in this lesson.

EXERCISES TO LESSON LXVI, PAGE 211.
Harmonizing of Florid Melodies.

1ª ORIGINAL. Melody given.

1ᵇ simplified.

2ª Melody given.

72

2ᵇ simplified.

3ᵃ Melody given.

3ᵇ simplified.

5b. Simplified.

6a. Bass given.

6b. Simplified.

7a.

7b. Simplified.

8a.

8b. Simplified.

LESSON LXVII, PAGE 213.
Accompaniments.

EXERCISES TO LESSON LXVIII, PAGE 218.
The Chromatic Scale Harmonized.

1. Ascending.

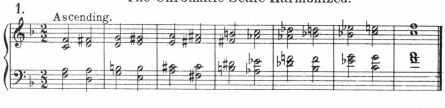

2.

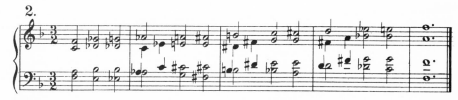

3.

EXERCISES TO LESSON LXIX, PAGE 221.

The Figured Chorale.

1. Melody in the Soprano.

2.

3.

4.

5. In triple rhythm.

EXERCISES TO LESSON LXX, PAGE 224.

The Figured Chorale. *(Continued.)*

Ia. Melody in the Bass.

1b. With passing tones, etc.

1c. In triple rhythm.

2 a.

2 b. With passing tones, etc.

In triple rhythm.

EXERCISES TO LESSON LXXI, PAGE 225.
The Figured Chorale.(*Continued.*)

1ª Melody in the Alto.

1b With nonharmonic tones,etc:

1c. And in triple rhythm:

2a. Melody in the Tenor.

2b. With nonharmonic tones, etc:

2c   And with triple rhythm.

EXERCISES TO LESSON LXXII, PAGE 227.
Analysis.

SIGNS USED IN ANALYSIS.

O.	Accented Passing Tone.	S.	Suspension.
+.	Unaccented Passing Tone.	F. T.	Free Tone.
App.	Appoggiatura.	E.	Embellishment.
D. App.	Double Appoggiatura.	O. P.	Organ Point.
Ant.	Anticipation.	T. O. P.	Tonic Organ Point.
F. Ant.	Free Anticipation.	D. O. P.	Dominant Organ Point.
R.	Retardation.		

Note: It will be seen by the following analysis that even dominant and diminished seventh chords are not considered as producing modulation unless followed by a more or less emphatic cadence in the same key. See Note 2, Lesson 72.

BACH.

1.

2. Andante cantabile.

MOZART.

+) These four counts may also be interpreted : $C:V_6^{?}$ I $g:VII^{\circ}{}_{70}$ I; which is the oldfash-
ioned interpretation, in contradistinction to the more modern idea of regarding such passages as intensifications of scale chords other than the tonic by associating them with their
apparent dominant or diminished sevenths, these apparent tonics being subordinate to the
tonic chord which fixes the key at the end of the phrase. In the above case the impression
of a change of key is very fleeting; hence the use of altered chords.

WAGNER.

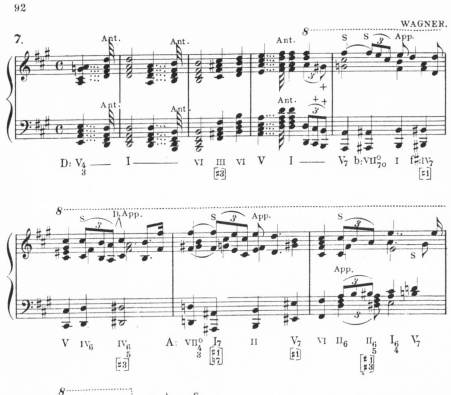

CHORAL MELODIES TO BE HARMONIZED, PAGE 231.

The following are taken from the 371 Choralgesänge by John Sebastian Bach. It is not expected that the pupil will succeed in harmonizing these chorales with the masterly daring and freedom of that great master, but he will gain much benefit from comparing his work with the originals.

1. Christ lag in Todesbanden.

2. Jesu, der du meine Seele.

3. Hilf, Herr Jesu, lass gelingen.

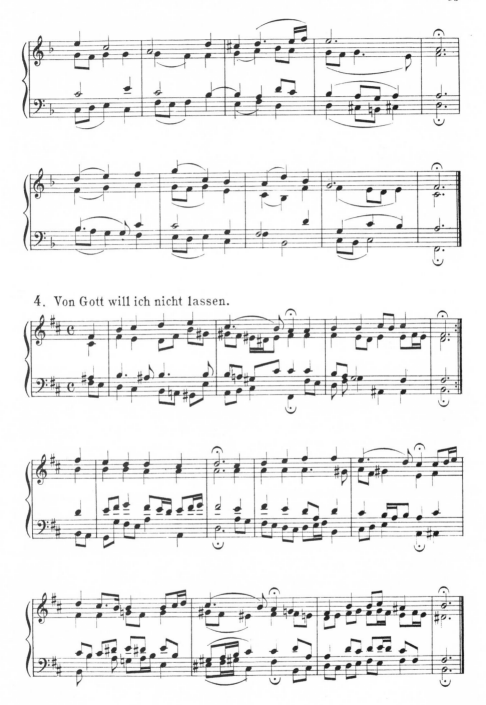

4. Von Gott will ich nicht lassen.

5. Allein zu dir, Herr Jesu Christ.

6. Meine Seel' erhebt den Herren.

7. Wenn mein Stündlein vorhanden ist.

8. **Lobt Gott, ihr Christen allzugleich.**

9. **Jesus, meine Zuversicht.**

10. Für deinen Thron tret' ich hiermit.

11. Liebster Jesu, wir sind hier.

12. Mit Fried' und Freud' ich fahr' dahin.

13. Wie schön leuchtet der Morgenstern.

14. Hilf, Gott, dass mir's gelinge.

15. Eins ist noth! ach Herr, dies Eine.

16. Herzlich lieb hab' ich dich, o Herr.

17. Vater unser im Himmelreich.

The exercises in this book may be reviewed with advantage by reharmonizing all the given melodies with modulations and suspensions. It is also recommended that the voice parts be written in

the vocal clefs, viz: Soprano ⣿ Alto ⣿ Tenor ⣿ and Bass ⣿ also for the string quartet:

1st Violin ⣿ 2d Violin ⣿ Viola ⣿ and 'Cello ⣿